ENDORSEMENTS

"Dr. Thomas Harrison is an encouragement machine! His words leap off the page, nurturing and empowering the reader to believe in the greatness of what can be. His wisdom and insight into the workings of the heart are a Godsend to those in need of hope and refreshment. Get this book and be blessed!"

Pastor Nick Rogers
District Youth Director
Executive Director, Roaring Springs Camp & Retreat Center
West Texas District of the Assemblies of God

"I cannot think of a better person to call when I need encouragement than Thomas Harrison. Not only is he an uplifting voice who speaks life into you, but he also provides a wealth of valuable information and insight helping to bring clarity to any situation you may encounter.

The book you hold in your hand will provide the oxygen for the soul we all need—encouragement. Breathe every page in deeply and get ready to have the fire rekindled in your soul."

Eric B. Smith
Destiny Church
Dayton, Ohio

"*Oxygen For The Soul* is a profound and timely work that speaks with clarity, compassion, and insight to the deeper needs of the human spirit. Dr. Thomas Harrison explores the essential practices and reflections that nourish the inner soul in an increasingly chaotic world.

As a dear friend, I admire Dr. Harrison's unwavering faith, integrity, wisdom, and heart for others. His ability to draw from both scholarly knowledge and lived experience offers readers not only practical insight but also genuine encouragement.

Oxygen For The Soul is definitely a book to read for those seeking spiritual renewal, adaptive resilience, and a deeper faith in God."

Bishop John K. Vincent
Greater Compassion Ministries Church
Nashville, Tennessee

"Thomas, I love the way you contribute yourself to helping and encouraging untold numbers of lives with your caring heart. And whosoever will be chief among you, let him be your servant: (Matthew 20:27)"

David Ingles
davidinglesmusic.org

"*Oxygen For The Soul* is a gentle breath of grace for weary hearts. Through true stories of kindness, faith, and quiet miracles, Dr. Thomas Harrison weaves a tapestry of hope drawn from the lives of ordinary people.

Each story is a whisper of God's presence—still healing, still moving, still writing beauty into broken places.

Whether you're leading, caregiving, dreaming, or simply holding on, this book offers what its name promises: soul-deep encouragement to help you keep going, keep believing, and keep loving—one story at a time."

Justin Cox
The Signature Group
Chattanooga, Tennessee

"I've had the privilege of knowing Thomas Harrison for several years. He's not only a gifted author but an incredibly talented and inspiring individual as well. His passion, creativity and heart—reflected so clearly in his writing—played a big role in inspiring me to become an author.

Oxygen For The Soul is exactly what the title promises—life-giving, faith-filled encouragement that breathes hope into weary hearts. Each page feels like a gentle reminder that no matter how hard things get, God is near, and His grace is enough.

Good books like this aren't just meant to be read, they're meant to be shared. After you finish this amazing book, I encourage you to pass it along or tell someone about it. You never know who might need the hope, encouragement, and life-giving truth found in these pages. Let this book be a gift not just for you, but for others as well."

Greg Wheat
Author, *From Here To There:*
Getting From Where You Are To Where You're Meant To Be

"The most encouraging person you know needs encouragement. Instilling confidence and security in others is what encouragers do. Encouragement inspires someone to pursue something, overcome obstacles, and tackle challenges. Everyone needs encouragement.

Dr. Thomas Harrison is an excellent communicator, professor, mentor, and friend, who personifies encouragement. When I read the moving stories in his previous book, *Move Up! Don't Give Up*, I immediately discovered relatable stories and experienced encouragement and helpful insights.

His new book, *Oxygen For The Soul*, is a must-read that will encourage you time and time again, doubtless when you need it most."

Mike McGinnis
The Christian Influence Podcast

"It won't come as a surprise for you to learn that growing up as the daughter of an evangelist who preached all over the world, I met lots of people. Oh my goodness, I was deluged with people, almost always being introduced as my father's daughter. It was actually a rare event when someone offered my first name. They just pointed to me and said: "This is Oral Roberts' daughter!" As you can imagine, such was not always that pleasant.

And perhaps that's one of the countless reasons I treasure my friendship with Dr. Thomas Harrison. It is his special care and concern for each and every individual — looking beyond what the world sees or cares about and noticing the needs perhaps unseen and deeply buried on the inside.

While oh so many of us go our merry way seeking our own fortunes or rush around so quickly perhaps to keep from getting hurt again, Thomas goes *his* way seeking those he can encourage, those he can help return to the land of the living. So if you feel a little beaten down today, perhaps a little out of breath from being stomped upon, know this. You have not come upon this book by accident.

I believe *Oxygen For The Soul* is an instrument which the Lord Jesus Christ has placed in your hands for this moment. I believe He will use it as His instrument to help you, to heal you, to bring you to the place He has called you to be. Believe that as you read it. And remember what Jesus said: ...Without me you can do nothing but ... with God all things are possible. John 15:5; Matthew 19:26 NKJV"

Roberta Roberts Potts

"It is a rare and powerful thing to find a man whose strength is matched by his gentleness, whose wisdom is deep but never distant, and whose leadership is rooted in love. Dr. Thomas Harrison is that kind of man. He understands the true value of relationships — not as a strategy, but as a calling. His life and message remind us that if we want to grow, mentorship is not optional — it's essential.

Thomas helps us recognize the power of spiritual fathering and relational accountability, showing us not only how to find a mentor but how to *become* one. His words are not just insightful — they're alive with conviction, compassion, and clarity. He equips people to find and walk in their purpose with a steady hand and a shepherd's heart.

As a friend, I've watched him pour into others with unwavering faithfulness, never seeking the spotlight, but always leaving a mark.

If you're seeking guidance or feel the call to guide others, the wisdom and spirit of Dr. Thomas Harrison will not only inspire you — it will *shape you*."

Jerry Edmon
Family Worship Center
Elgin, Texas

"Dr. Thomas Harrison's mentorship over the years has sustained me in some of my darkest times. He truly has a caring heart, and he is more than a person of words. He is one of action. We need more people like Thomas in our world."

Lee Guidry, Ed.D.
Associate Professor
Nelson University

"Before I even knew the topic of Thomas' new book, I suspected it would be about encouragement, whether for oneself or to give to another. Lo and behold, I was right! Thomas chose the topic of encouragement, because that's who he is and that's what he does every day.

I think of *Oxygen For The Soul* as *oxygen therapy* for those wanting to improve their overall health and quality of life."

David Warren
Program Director
Oasis Radio Network

"I think of *Oxygen For The Soul* as oxygen therapy for those wanting to improve their overall health and quality of life."
David Warren, *Oasis Radio Network*

OXYGEN FOR THE SOUL

Life is too short to be discouraged

Featuring encouraging articles from Stan Toler, Richard Exley, David Ingles, Roberta Roberts Potts, Jerry Edmon, Myles Holmes, and others.

Thomas Harrison, Ph.D.

FROM THE AUTHOR OF *MOVE UP! DON'T GIVE UP!*

Foreword by Richard Exley

Oxygen For The Soul: Life Is Too Short To Be Discouraged

Published by Dust Jacket Press
ISBN Paperback: 978-1-953285-78-2
ISBN Hardback: 978-1-953285-93-5

Dust Jacket Press
P.O. Box 721243
Oklahoma City, OK 73172
www.dustjacket.com

Edited by Roberta Roberts Potts and Roberta's Research - robertajpottslaw@icloud.com
Cover design by Madi Harper - madiharpart.com
Interior design by D.E. West - emoondesigns.com w/ Dust Jacket Press Creative Services
Photography: *Back Cover Photo:* Bill Shackelford
Inside Photos: Christina Bullard, Nancy Fauth,
Kathy Harrison, Rodney Hutcheson, Tim Maroney,
Michael McGinnis, Nick Rogers, Joshua Somma,
Teddy Wyatt, Cory Zollo

Printed in the United States

DEDICATION

Oxygen For The Soul
is dedicated to
my spiritual sons and daughters.
Past. Present. Future.

Each of you, in your own way,
have blessed me as I have encouraged,
and continue to encourage and strengthen
the Kingdom of God—worldwide.

May God's favor be upon you.
May signs and wonders follow your work
in the name of the Lord Jesus Christ.

May you accomplish things I cannot.
May you minister to those I cannot.

May you find your voice and place
in academia, commerce, leadership, ministry, and
in areas I cannot begin to imagine or comprehend.

As you do these things,
I will be blessed, encouraged, and well-pleased!

I am proud of you!

I have no greater joy than this,
to hear that my (spiritual) children
are living (their lives) in the truth.
3 John 1:4 AMP

CONTENTS

FOREWORD

Well, it has been said, "There is none so blind as he who won't see." Sometimes I feel like that when I'm around Thomas Harrison because we may be looking at the same thing, but he sees things I do not see, at least I do not see them until he points them out! That's his gift. He has a way of seeing into the heart of things, a way of seeing into our hearts, and his writing helps us to see what he sees.

Maybe he sees more clearly because he cares more deeply. I believe it was Augustine who was asked, "What does love look like?" He answered: "Love has hands to help others. It has feet to hasten to the poor and needy. **It has eyes to see misery and want.** It has ears to hear the sighs and sorrow of men. That is what love looks like" (emphasis mine).

Thomas not only has eyes to see misery and want, but also eyes to see beauty in the most unlikely places, and hope and possibilities too. His personal stories, insightful observations, and inspiring vignettes give us eyes to see what he sees and faith to believe. As inspiring as his vision is, as encouraging and uplifting as his writing is, it is only part of his gift, a small part. His greatest gift is his heart.

Let me explain. My wife and I were married for 56 years and when she went to be with Jesus I grieved unspeakably. Ordinary tasks seemed overwhelming. I never told anyone, but Thomas seemed to sense my struggle. Instead of just praying for me (which he did), or simply sending a card or a note, he telephoned me. Over my protests he insisted on driving nearly three hours to spend a day and a half helping with things that needed doing. Several tasks were labor intensive, but he never complained. How was it Augustine put it? "Love has hands to help others."

I guess what I'm trying to say is that Thomas lives what he writes. He's the real deal and so is *Oxygen For The Soul*. Get a copy for yourself and several for your friends. They will thank you for it.

Richard Exley
Author and Speaker

INTRODUCTION

While searching and praying for a subtitle for *Oxygen For The Soul*, my editor and I exchanged what seemed to be endless suggestions. Each one was close, but not close enough.

One day my editor was running errands and noticed a truck for a service company which had a similar slogan. With some rewrite, the subtitle was born.

The struggle for the subtitle is similar to what many people struggle with; they are missing *something* but are not sure what that *something* may be. Some turn to drugs, alcohol, self-destructing activities, while others may think the *something* is found in work, exotic travel, accumulating wealth, or hoarding material possessions.

The truth is that *something* is actually two elements: *someone* and *something*. Without *a sustaining faith in Jesus*, we cannot see God. Without *encouragement*, life is barely worth the effort.

Oxygen For The Soul is my mission to encourage as many as I can. I hope to rekindle your faith in God and the belief that He wants you to live a purposeful life...and life "to the full" as John 10:10 proclaims.

Encouragement is oxygen to the soul.
George Madison Adams

Have you ever noticed when someone compliments you, the words stay with you? They help you to stand taller, feel better, and you seem to have the energy to continue with a new resolve.

Oxygen For The Soul picks up where *Move Up! Don't Give Up!* left off, developing deeper truths — proving that encouragement changes not only the atmosphere—but people, families, generations, and even nations.

Although not intentional, you will discover this book is partly biographical. You will learn what I value and hold near as a part of my belief system. Among my favorite things in life is my love for southern cooking, Chick-fil-A, handwritten thank-you notes, teaching and administration in undergraduate and graduate higher education, classic and vintage cars, hymns, ministry, as well as friends and family. My favorite times are when I am mentoring in a one-on-one meeting. My love for the eternal truth of God's Word and my Savior, Jesus Christ, the gifts and manifestations of the Holy Spirit as well as God's creation of us and how He uses us to accomplish His plans will become clear.

Recurring values portrayed in this text that are closest to me are those of friendship, loyalty, peace, hard work, service to others, and mentorship. At the core of who I am is someone who wants everyone to succeed and become better versions of themselves.

The reader will meet members of my family, friends, fellow ministers, and spiritual sons and daughters; many with whom I have shared radio and television interview programs, internet news podcasts, pulpits, ministry assignments, and other projects. I have been guests in their homes as well. A few I have traveled and conducted seminars with — and some have traveled with me for times of ministry or recreation.

While we are on the subject of the contributors of the second section of *Oxygen For The Soul*, the roster reads like my Christmas card list. I would not present to you random individuals with whom I have no relationship and who do not share my values and mission. Oh, how I would enjoy assembling these servant-ministers in one place for you to meet and come to know as I do.

My best friend is the one who brings out the best in me.

Henry Ford

Oxygen For The Soul has not been without its challenges, as one would expect with any literary endeavor. Yet my load has become lighter thanks to a group of friends who helped bring out the best in me.

Kathy Harrison has been my supporter and cheerleader through this project and in life. The reader will see her influence in many of the stories in this book. If there ever were a Proverbs 31 woman, it is my wife of 46 years, Kathy Harrison.

Roberta Roberts Potts of Roberta's Research has served in a repeat performance as my editor for this second book. My friend always had my best interest as she edited page after page. With her insight came wisdom and understanding of my dream. Often her edits would contain correction and encouragement. Thank you, Roberta, for bringing out the best in me and my writing. Roberta's work with my manuscripts reminds me of something Adrienne Posey said, "Further editing deepens a story."

Adam Toler of DustJacket Press, my publisher. Always the ultimate professional, Adam has guided me through two book projects. Seth Godin describes the ideal publisher, and I would also describe Adam with these words. "The future of publishing is about having connections to readers and the knowledge of what those readers want." Thank you, Adam, for believing in me!

My Dear Reader, thank you for taking this journey to discover a transformative world of encouragement. As you read each page, each story, each article, may God renew within you a sense of rejoicing, purpose, and blessing.

Therefore encourage one another with these words…
1 Thessalonians 4:18 NIV

Thomas Harrison, Ph.D.
February 1, 2026

A SECRET AGENT'S MISSION

He sat in a booth next to the window. A man in his 70's or 80's caught my attention. He was quietly eating alone; unnoticed by all around him. Without hesitation, I excused myself from our family meal and quietly made my way to the register.

The owner of my favorite hole-in-the-wall fish restaurant* recognizes me and asks what he can do to help.

"See the man by the window, eating alone…I want to buy his dinner…and it's our secret," I said convincingly. "You are talking about Devin; he's eating the small fish plate…$11.67" replied the owner. He is familiar enough with my routine. I leave a nice tip and return to our table.

My heart melts when I see people eating alone, especially seniors. I determined years ago that while I can't share a meal with these lone diners—I could buy their meal—in secret.

Pure and undefiled religion before God the Father is this: to care for orphans and widows in their adversity and to keep oneself unstained by the world.
James 1:27 NET

For a moment, I am part Secret Agent, part Angelic Messenger—a servant of God using my resources to help another soul experience an unexpected gift of grace—a free meal.

As we were leaving, the owner said to me, "You made his day. Thank you!"

This is not a random act of kindness. It is a planned and purposeful blessing.

I share this encounter to encourage you to find your own secret mission. You can be God's Secret Agent and Angelic Messenger—bringing God's grace to a lonely soul. While your mission will change the life of your unsuspecting subjects—it will also change your heart and life. These blessing missions will encourage a generous spirit in those you enlist to assist you.

Who received the greater blessing that night? There were three lives that will never be the same.

**The Fish Shack, Coweta, Oklahoma*

THE LAST $25

In 1913, a Kansas family heard missionary accounts of people afflicted with leprosy.

The missionary explained how $25 could provide antibiotics for an afflicted person for one year.

The Chapman family agreed they would provide funds for ten patients. They began asking friends to help raise funds to pay their pledge for the cause.

Ten-year-old Wilbur Chapman was enthralled with these stories, and God moved on his heart. As the missionary left town, he gave Wilbur three silver dollars.

Wilbur had an idea to use his financial windfall to purchase a piglet and raise it to sell the pig to help the lepers.

After caring for and feeding the pig named Pete, Wilber sold the pig for $25. It was the final amount needed to complete the family's pledge.

After reading Wilbur's story, a woman in Virginia named Mrs. Harrison (doubtful of any relation to the author) had an idea to craft coin banks in the shape of a pig. She supplied them to the American Mission to Lepers (now known as Hope Rises International) as a fundraiser.

These Piggy Banks generated donations of one million dollars to the mission.

Wilbur's idea generated a return of 733 percent.

Even more impressive is the missionary's return on his $3 investment, which yielded 33,333,323 percent.

You can visit White Cloud, Kansas, and see the plaque commemorating Wilbur and the namesake of the Piggy Bank.

Can God use you, your idea, or your money? Most assuredly!

The plans of the diligent lead to profit as surely as haste leads to poverty.
Proverbs 21:5 AMP

Your creative idea may be the miracle someone is praying for.
Dr. Thomas Harrison

https://www.hmdb.org/m.asp?m=47396

A BROKEN SPIRIT

A merry heart does good like a medicine,
but a broken spirit dries the bones.
Proverbs 17:22 NKJV

I was discussing this scripture with my Christian physician one day, and he gave me new insight into this Biblical truth. “People love to quote the first part but ignore the second part.” It was his opinion that *dried bones* referred to arthritis. His theory was that a continual broken spirit brings about arthritis and other ailments as well.

The struggles of life may wound and break the spirit of a person.

Two of the most holy and righteous men in the Bible, Job and Elijah, had emotional crises which were so severe they asked God to take their lives—and immediately. (Job 6:8, 1 Kings 19:4; see also *Broken Down on Discouragement Street* found elsewhere in this book.)

We should do everything possible to encourage our spirit in a healthy way; prayer, Bible reading, meditation, reading good books, watching comedy movies, physical exercise, and talking with Christian friends—even counselors. Our mental health is as important as our physical health.

There are times when the therapies listed above do not resolve the inner turmoil of a broken spirit, at least not as quickly as you would like. If you, or someone you love, need professional mental healthcare, even medication, by all means seek such treatment.

You have cared for others; now is the time to care for yourself!

ENCOURAGEMENT IS OXYGEN TO THE BODY AND SPIRIT

When I attended Oral Roberts University, one of the non-academic requirements for graduation was to pass a series of physical fitness tests.

While running in preparation for a field test, we were required to run an indoor test within a certain time.

I was never athletic, but God had clearly spoken to me that I was to complete my bachelor's degree at ORU.

The coach divided the class into teams of two. One kept time while the other ran. As an experiment, the coach told us not to say anything to the runner on the first round. Beginning with the second round, shout encouragement to the runner each successive round.

One would think the more laps you ran, the more tired you would become, but actually, the successive laps were better time-wise than the first.

Years later I can see and hear my running partner, Tim, encouraging me to keep running.

I remember the feeling of accomplishment as I reviewed my results.

In the marathon we call life, let us encourage each other. It truly does make quite a difference.

Therefore encourage one another and build each other up...
1 Thessalonians 5:11 NIV

My mission in life is to encourage others, including you.

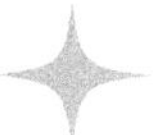

"I LEARNED SOMETHING FROM YOU!"

I sat on the couch in a 200+ year old home in Maine where my host had invited me for lunch.

My host had been generous to my employer and we met to discuss future giving opportunities.

This man was a retired minister whom God had blessed financially. He owns real estate, businesses and manages investments.

While talking about his work and giving, he told me: "I learned something from you!"

Stunned, I politely asked what I had taught him in my few—and brief—encounters.

"You have taught me the value of Thank You Notes!"

He stated that while he always thanked people in ministry and business—he regretted not sending handwritten Thank You Notes.

"Perhaps I could have done more…" he lamented.

My friend, let us not regret the opportunity to "do more."

I have not stopped giving thanks to God for you.
I remember you in my prayers.
Ephesians 1:16 GNT

"YOU DON'T HAVE ANY TROUBLE. ALL YOU NEED IS FAITH IN GOD."

This was the signature quotation of Evangelist R.W. Schambach, who was a client of mine at two radio stations I managed during my media career.

I will never forget a private lunch we had in Oklahoma City. What a genuine man full of God's love and humility.

When I arrived at his hotel to take him to the restaurant, I could not find him. Soon, I noticed he was witnessing to a custodian! I will always remember that picture of this man of faith.

This man inspired millions to trust God.

In his later years, he was known for his wisdom and sound judgment in the difficult situations which were presented to him.

Whatever you may be facing, remember God is FOR you and not against you.

But as for me, I will sing of Your strength; Yes, I will joyfully sing of Your faithfulness in the morning, For You have been my refuge And a place of refuge on the day of my distress. Psalm 59:16 NASB

For more information about the life and ministry of R.W. Schambach check this website schambachfoundation.org

Photo by Kathy Harrison

CARING IS THE NEW SUPERPOWER

While thankfully things now appear to be moving in a different direction, our nation has been experiencing rising prices, inflation, and unprecedented gasoline prices. The backlash from supply chain interruptions caused once abundant products to become scarce.

The good news is the Cost of Caring is not subject to inflation.

The Cost of Caring (C/C) is a process that measures the essential elements of caring and establishes an economic benefit of C/C in operation.

Stated: The Cost of Caring is free. It is void of any inflationary or market-reactive influence which would dilute its effects. Indeed, the Cost of Caring is a superpower.

"Caring is the act of displaying kindness and concern for another." (Oxford Dictionary)

In my working definition, caring is the art of displaying a quality we have traditionally deemed as intangible. While I may have concern for you, unless I *do something* with that concern, neither you nor I benefit. It is not until I put action with my thoughts and emotions that any benefit is derived.

Nothing changes until I say or do something to demonstrate my concern for your well-being.

Expressing concern for another is a noble act best demonstrated by thoughtful comments and actions with the expressed desire to bless, minister, or encourage another.

Caring is such a positive force with us that it abolishes negative emotions and vanquishes selfishness. It transforms us from prideful, selfish, egocentric humans and allows us to walk in the sensitive, thoughtful, generous image of God to which He called us.

Is it possible that in its purest form, caring can redeem a crestfallen soul? Could the act of caring be so powerful that it transforms both giver and receiver? Are the tangible demonstrations of caring so dynamic that in operation, others are influenced, and a micro-society experiences its effects?

Yes! Yes!! Yes!!!

The effects of caring are so powerful that while you read this article, your mind is racing and remembering times when you received the demonstration of caring from another. While you remember those events, you are further reminded of times when you demonstrated caring for another.

Caring is a chameleon, changing to fit the environment. In one stratum, caring is a smile or holding the door open for the next person. Other times caring involves a financial investment or physical activity.

Caring, in and of itself, is so powerful that nothing additional is needed. Encouragement compounds the effects of caring. How wonderful it is to care about someone, but even more significant to demonstrate concern for another by adding encouragement.

Caring is the new superpower.

As, therefore, God's picked representatives of the new humanity, purified and beloved of God himself, be merciful in action, kindly in heart, humble in mind. Accept life, and be most patient and tolerant with one another, always ready to forgive if you have a difference with anyone. Forgive as freely as the Lord has forgiven you. And, above everything else, be truly loving, for love is the golden chain of all the virtues. Colossians 3:12-14 Phillips

ALL THE MONEY IN THE WORLD?

When I have been asked, "If you had all the money in the world, what would you do?" my answer has always been, "I would give everyone in the world a job!"

While on assignment in McAllen, Texas deep in the Rio Grande Valley, friends took me to Reynosa, Mexico. I noticed the poor, street vendors and shop owners.

The street vendors (even if only a cardboard box) seemed happier than those who were begging.

The store operators (even if only makeshift storefronts) seemed happier, even wealthy, compared to street vendors.

Whatever our circumstances, we are blessed beyond measure.

... I have learned how to be content with whatever I have. I know how to live on almost nothing or with everything. I have learned the secret of living in every situation, whether it is with a full stomach or empty, with plenty or little. For I can do everything through Christ, who gives me strength. Philippians 4:11-13 NLT

BELIEVE GOD FOR THE IMPOSSIBLE

In 2014 my friend, Pastor Eric Smith, took a leap of faith and rented Memorial Hall, a municipal auditorium in Dayton, Ohio. He invited two world-renowned ministers to join him: John Kilpatrick and Lindell Cooley.

Their meeting began on Pentecost Sunday in the same building Aimee Semple McPherson preached to overflow crowds in 1920.

Eric took a step of faith, believing God for big things!

So also, Abraham "believed God, and it was credited to him as righteousness." Understand, then, that those who have faith are children of Abraham. Scripture foresaw that God would justify the Gentiles by faith, and announced the gospel in advance to Abraham: "All nations will be blessed through you." So those who rely on faith are blessed along with Abraham, the man of faith. Galatians 3:6-9 NIV

We are children of Abraham.

Believe God for big things in your life.

Do something which only God can help you accomplish.

I am inspired by my friend Eric and others who are believing God for the miraculous.

Pastor Eric provided this update to this message which I sent to my network on June 8, 2014:

"I find that people still talk about those meetings. We had about 75 different local pastors attend the meetings, and about 600-700 people nightly. Visitors from as far away as Seattle, Washington. We had many touched with God's power, experience healing, Holy Spirit baptism, and other encounters with God. Brother Kilpatrick released a powerful prophetic word for Dayton, Ohio that I still have a copy of. The meetings did a lot to bring unity to the Body of Christ here in the Dayton area as well as strengthen and build my relationships with the pastors in the area."

Watch the video documentary about this momentous occasion!

https://youtu.be/R2fG_ch93-o?si=bg3usBN1-dBojssc

DR. HARRISON'S WORDS OF WISDOM

"A wise man asks:
"Who will pay for this? How much does it cost?"

"Appreciate the gift. Disregard the packaging."

"Do not grieve over what God has delivered you from."

"Earn the right to speak."

"Exceptional leaders extend their confidence, expertise, and excellence to those around them."

"Find someone you believe in, then push and promote them!

If you are not pushing and promoting someone, then find someone to encourage! So many people are waiting for someone to believe in them."

"Fear keeps us from hearing the voice of God which brings us good news."

"Foolishness leads godly people to
a path of destruction."

"Forgiveness is the only path forward
after a wounded spirit."

"God does not consult your past to determine your future.
Neither should you."

"Grace is something we all crave.
Give grace whenever possible."

"Honoring God is the first rule of success."

"I have never cried over spilled milk. Ever.
Spilled Chick-fil-A Sweet Tea is another matter."

"If you don't know where you are going;
any road will take you there."

"If you think you know everything,
no one can help you."

"If you want to read me, look at my friends and
spiritual sons and daughters. Then you will know
who I am and what I believe."

"If we can see beauty in the ugly, we have an understanding of forgiveness and redemption."

"In the absence of rules, people make their own."

"Keep the old behind you and the new ahead of you."

"Let us be thankful for:

What we have,

What we do not have,

And what does not have us."

"Love on people, train them, give them opportunities, and let them fly! They will in turn follow you anywhere."

"Speak to the hurt and you will always have an attentive audience."

"My friend, I believe in you! God and I are on your side!

If you have failed, or you are not sure you have done your best, the word I have for you today is: I give you permission to find the power to redo this."

"Never doubt yourself."

"We never know how one thing can prepare us for another thing which will occur in our future."

"People are too busy doing their jobs;
they don't think to do their job well."

"If we spend our lives encouraging people,
we will never want for a ministry—we will BE ministry."

"Photos sell and tell the story."

"Procrastination comes to all who wait for it."

"Serving others is the hallmark of a Christ-follower and
the basic requirement for leadership."

"Sometimes you need to go to a safe place to
allow God's healing to come to you."

"The best thing you can do for yourself is to help someone."

"The inability to communicate has silenced many
brilliant people, and unfortunately, has sidelined them
from action and accomplishment."

"Most people want to fly. They just need someone
to show them how and then encourage them to soar."

"The prayers of mighty men of God are included
in the Bible, not by their publicists; but are the direction
of the Holy Spirit to build our faith."

"The secret of happiness and prosperity is in blessing others."

"The secret to success in life is not how little you can give,

but in how much you can invest."

"The world is waiting for someone like you
to do the work only you can do."

"We have the choice to live the dream or toss the dream.
Do not be a dream tosser."

"The best gifts to give are ourselves and then our resources."

"We never know the torment and grief others face and hide."

"What if the next project you created would change the world?

Approach every project with excellence and purpose."

"When inspiration comes, arise and write."

"Wherever your journeys are taking you during
this season of life—REJOICE—God is taking good care
of you! He knows the path. Trust your guide."

"You are worthy of the love you crave."

"Your next idea may be the answer to someone's prayer."

Photo by Rodney Hutcheson

BROKEN-DOWN ON DISCOURAGEMENT STREET

In Zarephath, Elijah prayed for a poor woman and a miraculous provision came to her house. On another occasion, the prophet prayed, and a young man was brought back to life. On Mount Carmel, Elijah literally called fire down from heaven to consume a sacrifice, and the prophets of Baal were killed.

Elijah later heard a report that the queen issued a warrant for his death.

Upon hearing this news, Elijah hid in a cave and asked God to take his life.

One of the most holy and righteous men of God asked God to take him to heaven--and quickly.

On life's journey, we may pass Discouragement Street. None of us are immune from discouragement.

True victory comes from God by the power of the Holy Spirit.

We are hard-pressed on every side, yet not crushed; we are perplexed, but not in despair; persecuted, but not forsaken; struck down, but not destroyed. 2 Corinthians 4: 8-9 NKJV

Should you find yourself broken down on Discouragement Street, please call a friend.

That is not a neighborhood you should travel through without a friend.

(This excerpt is from my message: *"Has God Forgotten You?"*)

HELPERS HIGH

Those who know the joy of serving others understand the benefits of putting others first. Science has finally confirmed what God taught us long ago.

> *"Researchers spend a lot of time debating whether any altruistic act is ever truly selfless because we benefit so much when we are kind to others. I think of kindness like laughter: we might be laughing because we want someone else to feel good about their joke, but mostly we laugh because it feels good. Like laughter, kindness is a terrific happiness habit, good for both our physical and emotional well-being...*
>
> *...volunteering is nearly as beneficial to our health as quitting smoking!*
>
> *We feel so good when we give because we get what researchers call a "helpers high," or a distinct physical sensation associated with helping."*
>
> Christine L. Carter, Ph.D.
> *Psychology Today*
> February 19, 2010

Give generously and generous gifts will be given back to you, shaken down to make room for more. Abundant gifts will pour out upon you with such an overflowing measure that it will run over the top! Your measurement of generosity becomes the measurement of your return. Luke 6:38 TPT

https://www.psychologytoday.com/us/blog/raising-happiness/201002/what-we-get-when-we-give

ENCOURAGEMENT: LINE BY LINE

"A cheerful disposition is good for your health;
gloom and doom leave you bone-tired."

Proverbs 17:22 MSG

"And this is the confidence that we have in him,
that, if we ask anything according to his will, he heareth us:
And if we know that he hears us, whatsoever we ask,
we know that we have the petitions that we desired of him."

1 John 5:14-15 KJV

"The prospect of the righteous is joy."

Proverbs 10:28 NIV

"An honest witness can save your life..."

Proverbs 14:25 CEV

"I sought the LORD, and He answered me and delivered me from all my fears. Those who look to Him are radiant, and their faces shall never be ashamed. Oh, taste and see that the LORD is good! Blessed is the man who takes refuge in Him!"

Psalm 34:4,5, 8 ESV

"We are troubled on every side, yet not distressed;

we are perplexed, but not in despair; persecuted, but not forsaken; cast down, but not destroyed."

II Corinthians 4: 8, 9 KJV

"As for me, I will always have hope; I will praise you more and more."

Proverbs 7:14 NIV

"Blessed be God, which hath not turned away my prayer, nor his mercy from me."

Psalm 66:20 KJV

"But you, my friends, keep on building yourselves up on your most sacred faith. Pray in the power of the Holy Spirit."

Jude 1:20 GNT

"The righteous choose their friends carefully."

Proverbs 12:26 NIV

"First plant your fields; then build your barn."

Proverbs 24:27 MSG

"For the LORD shall be thy confidence,
and shall keep thy foot from being taken."

Proverbs 3:26 KJV

"God has not given us the spirit of fear;
but of power, and of love, and of a sound mind."

II Timothy 1:7 KJV

"Humility and the fear of the Lord brings wealth
and honor and life."

Proverbs 22:4 NIV

"I'll refresh tired bodies; I'll restore tired souls."

Jeremiah 31:25 MSG

"In the (reverent) fear of the LORD there is strong confidence.
And His children will (always) have a place of refuge."

Proverbs 14:26 AMP

"My thoughts are filled with beautiful words for the king,
And I will use my voice as a writer uses pen and ink."

Psalm 45:1 CEV

"I wisdom dwell with the prudent and find
out knowledge of witty inventions."

Proverbs 8:12 KJV

"As we have therefore opportunity, let us do good unto all men, especially unto them who are of the household of faith."

Galatians 6: 10 KJV

❖

"Know that the Lord has set apart the godly for himself, the Lord will hear when I call to him."

Psalm 4:3 NIV

❖

"Learn to do good; seek justice, correct oppression; bring justice to the fatherless, plead the widow's cause."

Isaiah 1:17 NIV

"No harm befalls the righteous."

Proverbs 12:21 NIV

"Let the favor of the Lord our God be upon us;
And confirm for us the work of our hearts;
Yes, confirm the work of our hands."

Psalm 90:17 NASB

"My brethren, count it all joy when ye fall into divers temptations; knowing this, That the trying of your faith worketh patience. But let patience have her perfect work, that ye may be perfect and entire, wanting nothing."

James 1: 2-4 KJV

"Let God grant what is in your heart and fulfill all your plans."

Psalm 20:4 CEB

"Oh my God, (please) remember me for good
(and imprint me on your heart)."

Nehemiah 13:31 AMP

"The lips of the righteous feed many."

Proverbs 10:21 KJV

"The Lord himself goes before you and will be with you;
He will never leave you nor forsake you.
Do not be afraid; do not be discouraged."

Deuteronomy 31:8 NIV

"A gift opens doors for a man and brings him before the great."

Proverbs 18:16 HCSB

"Do you see someone skilled in his work?
They will serve before kings;
they will not serve before obscure men."

Proverbs 22:29 NIV

"Never forget your leaders, who first spoke to you the Word of God.
Remember how they lived and imitate their faith."

Hebrews 13:7 Phillips

"The righteous man is rescued from trouble."
Proverbs 11:8 NIV

"The Lord is a stronghold for the oppressed,
a stronghold in times of trouble."

Psalm 9:9 ESV

"A stingy man is eager to get rich and
is unaware that poverty awaits him."
Proverbs 28:22 NIV

"The Lord is near to the brokenhearted
and saves the crushed in spirit."

Psalm 34:18 ESV

"They do not fear bad news;
they confidently trust the Lord to care for them."

Psalm 112:7 NLT

"Whoever isolates himself seeks his own desire;
he breaks out against all sound judgment."

Proverbs 18:1 ESV

BUILDING A LEGACY

"Ministry is expressed in various forms; listening is essential, talking and acting are secondary." Dr. Thomas Harrison

When I moved to Oklahoma, God spoke these words to my heart, "You will be a friend to pastors." It was not something I asked for, but I gladly accepted the mantle, readily understanding that the life of a pastor, while fulfilling in many ways can also be lonely and more than arduous.

One day I was lunching with a dear pastor friend who picked up my mantle of leadership of a regional pastors' prayer gathering in the Tulsa, Oklahoma area. This monthly meeting of pastors has met for more than 30 years.

I talked a while back with a Christian businessman who sold his 65-year-old business and is presently helping the new owners expand.

We build a legacy one day at a time, one relationship at a time, one accomplishment at a time.

We may struggle, fail, fight for what is right, or move from glory to glory. The key is to keep moving.

Wherever you are, whatever you are doing, keep working and trusting God. The work you do is more important than you may know. You touch more lives than you can imagine. Your work is more important than you realize. The legacy you are building and will leave to another one day is too important for you to give up.

...Rise up and build. Nehemiah 2:18 KJV

CHRISTMAS BELLS

I heard the bells on Christmas day
Their old familiar carols play,
And wild and sweet the words repeat
Of peace on earth, good will to men.

I thought how, as the day had come,
The belfries of all Christendom
Had rolled along th'unbroken song
Of peace on earth, good will to men.

And in despair I bowed my head:
"There is no peace on earth," I said,
"For hate is strong, and mocks the song
Of peace on earth, good will to men."

Then pealed the bells more loud and deep:
"God is not dead, nor doth He sleep;
The wrong shall fail, the right prevail,
With peace on earth, good will to men."

Till, ringing, singing on its way,
The world revolved from night to day
A voice, a chime, a chant sublime,

Of peace on earth, good will to men.

I Heard The Bells On Christmas Day
Henry Wadsworth Longfellow (1864)

Noted poet, Henry Wadsworth Longfellow, wrote a poem titled *Christmas Bells*. Originally, it speaks of the state of the world in a hopeful fashion, but then in verse four, tragedy and despair strike. Finding the hope he was seeking, the author moves to conclude the song in jubilant triumph over evil.

I understand the backstory to this song is that Longfellow's personal world had fallen apart.

In our own lives, may we find peace and hope in our God during all seasons.

Now may the God of peace make you holy in every way, and may your whole spirit and soul and body be kept blameless until our Lord Jesus Christ comes again.
1 Thessalonians 5:23 NLT

Hymnary.org is my primary research website for lyrics, author biography, and history of sacred music.

GOD LEADS US ALONG

In shady, green pastures, so rich and so sweet,
God leads His dear children along;
Where the water's cool flow bathes the weary one's feet,
God leads His dear children along.

Refrain:

Some through the waters, some through the flood,
Some through the fire, but all through the blood;
Some through great sorrow, but God gives a song,
In the night season and all the day long.

God Leads Us Along
G.A. Young (1903)

...God my Maker, who gives us songs in the night.
Job 35:10 BSB

Hymnary.org is my primary research website for lyrics, author biography, and history of sacred music.

NEED AN ENERGY BOOST?

When my grandfather was feeling low or not as healthy as usual, he had a sure-fire remedy for whatever was ailing him.

On these occasions, he shaved using a double-edge safety razor and a metal wash basin, using water he heated on the kitchen stove. He would then drive to a nursing home or hospital to visit patients to encourage them.

He seldom knew those he visited. "I always feel better when I leave than when I came. I am free to come and go; these people aren't as mobile as I am."

I have found the same joy in making hospital calls as my grandfather.

There is something about helping people that energizes me.

Perhaps you too need an energy (and spiritual) boost?

I telephoned an aged minister to wish him "Happy Birthday." He said his wife tells people of my kindness helping him walk up and down off the platform when he was having mobility issues.

(A one-time event, a courtesy I extended during a ministry service.)

When a friend has a family member who dies, the tradition in our home is to mail a sympathy card and a copy of the book *When You Lose Someone You Love* by Richard Exley. We have mailed hundreds of these through the years. We always have a supply on hand to bless our friends.

I share these things with you to encourage you to find something you can do for someone to bless them.

And let us bestow thought on one another with a view to arousing one another to brotherly love and right conduct.
Hebrews 10:24 Weymouth

And if I have the gift of prophecy, and know all mysteries and all knowledge; and if I have all faith, so as to remove mountains, but have not love, I am nothing.
1 Corinthians 13:2 ERV

EVERYONE IS DIFFERENT EXCEPT ME AND THEE

My wife's grandmother who lived to be 100 years old, had a quaint saying about the differences in people.

"Everyone is different except me and thee; Except thee takes cream in thy tea."

We live in a world where the expression of self-image takes many forms. Some healthy; others destructive.

While managing a Christian television station in Tulsa, Oklahoma, we had an annual outreach hosting a booth at the Tulsa State Fair. It was fun but lots of work.

One day a man began an argument with me about evolution. While I knew many facts, I soon realized I was in over my head and beyond my scope of knowledge.

We have all been there. Wishing, hoping, praying for a way out.

From seemingly nowhere, a man enters our conversation and it is obvious he is a believer in Jesus. He defends my position and begins to answer point-to-point this man's challenges to our faith.

I politely and discreetly removed myself.

Who was this man? I do not know. All I can remember now is that he wore a Guns N' Roses ball cap.

My angel and defender of the faith came wearing a Guns N' Roses ball cap?!? If I would have requested an angel, he might have worn a Gaither Vocal Band ball cap. After all, Guns N' Roses is known as the most dangerous band in the world.*

If I ever believed an angel was dispatched to protect me, this was the occasion. Perhaps the one who was attacking our faith could only have been reached by someone dressed in this manner. In any event, I believe I witnessed Psalm 91:11 that day: "For He will command His angels in regard to you. To protect and defend and guard you in all ways…" AMP

Pastor Billy Joe Daugherty of Tulsa, Oklahoma was gifted in talking to those who were different in appearance. He would often ask those whose hair was wild or unusually styled: "How do you get your hair to do that?" He said this line opened many doors for him to share the gospel.

When we encounter those who look and act differently, we can retreat as if threatened.

We can also ask for wisdom to understand and relate.

If any of you lack wisdom, let him ask of God,
that giveth to all men liberally, and upbraideth not;
and it shall be given him.
James 1:5 KJV

Whether you take cream in your tea, wear a Guns N' Roses ball cap, or style your hair to stand straight up—you are God's creation.

I am exuberantly proud of you, my friend.

*****https://en.wikipedia.org/wiki/Guns_N%27_Roses*

THANKFUL FOR THE "NOTS"

With contemporary society in a hectic pace to create and perpetuate materialism, this value often transfers to the spiritual side of life. For example, when we are asked to pause and think about the things for which we are thankful, we recite a litany of items that resemble an *inventory* rather than actual *blessings*. I am the first to admit my guilt to the former charge. On numerous occasions, I have recited countless *things* in an effort to sound *spiritual*.

Would you admit with me that our listing of *things* often turns to *one-upmanship*. We equate God's blessings in our lives with the things we can touch, hold, mortgage, invest, borrow, store, convert, guard, or hoard.

For once, I am thankful for the *nots* in my life. That's right! I am thankful for all the things that I do not have! These thoughts came to me one day as I prayed while driving to work.

- I am thankful for the things I did not say, for the times when God helped me to keep my tongue in check. Keeping my mouth shut has saved me from a flattened wallet, nose, or reputation. I practice the art and gift of patience.
- I am thankful for all the things I did not buy. All I need in my life are more *things*. After a while, no matter how much I think I need them, these *things* end up in my garage or my garage sale.

- I am thankful for all the job offers I did not accept. Some companies that offered me a job are no longer in business or are on a different life course than I am pursuing.
- I am thankful some of my thoughts did not become a reality. Imagination is a blessing and a curse. We are to take control over thoughts, especially those which challenge God's plan
- (2 Corinthians 10:5). Do you really want to *see* all of what your mind imagines?
- I am thankful I did not make decisions during emotional times. Fortunately, God allowed my blood pressure to settle down so I could make rational decisions after the heat of the moment passed. Never make decisions when you are hurting, afraid, lonely, or tired.
- I am thankful for all the ailments and diseases I did not contract. I am healthy. I know people who lack good health.
- I am thankful for all the people I did not refuse to help. Some needed help; for others, it was not as obvious. When I helped, I was the one who received the greater blessing.
- I am thankful for all the times I did not hesitate to speak a kind word or do a kind deed. My favorite *kindness* approach is to do something secretly.

Kind words cost nothing but yield significant dividends.

This message has been published in The Oklahoman and other newspapers.

YOU ARE THEIR SHEPHERD

If you meet regularly with people for lunch or activities, they are your tribe, and you are their shepherd. While the words of John 10:11 refer to Jesus, we are also called to be good shepherds. I suppose few would argue that many today are in fact like sheep without a shepherd. (Matthew 9:36)

You have a congregation God has given you to nurture, guide, instruct, and protect.

Pray for them on a regular basis. Ask God for wisdom. Allow the Holy Spirit to give you specific words of comfort, edification, or correction.

Do not proclaim your leadership, yet quietly and humbly be the guide they need.

FIVE WORDS STOPPED MY PLAN

During a church service, the minister's comments about technology and administration were unsettling to me. He even reinforced his remarks the following week with an illustration. Perhaps the minister was either frustrated or uninformed. I believed I should come to the rescue since I have a professional and educational background in those subjects.

The minister is someone I have a relationship with but felt I could not casually mention my concerns. Thus, I devised a plan to contact a member of the technology oversight committee I know and ask him to relay my concerns to the minister.

There was no doubt in my mind that my insights should be communicated, and thus all would be right with the world.

My wife was in both services and did not remember the comments. I told Kathy my plan.

"Did he ask your opinion?" she asked.

I sheepishly replied, "No."

She had insight into both the minister and her husband. Several days passed and I realized what a horrible plan this was.

I debated for several months if I should share this. Exposing my *stinking thinking* (as Zig Ziglar called it) is not something I enjoy. Perhaps you knew this lesson already.

Withholding our opinion is as much an art as it is a science. It is better to withhold an opinion than to ruin a friendship.

Never miss a good chance to shut up.
Will Rogers

A person that does not value your time
will not value your advice.
Orrin Woodward

Those who guard their mouths and their tongues
keep themselves from calamity.
Proverbs 21:23 NIV

GRACE IS EXCEPTIONAL

War is not exceptional; peace is.
Worry is not exceptional; trust is.
Decay is not exceptional; restoration is.
Anger is not exceptional; gratitude is.
Selfishness is not exceptional; sacrifice is.
Defensiveness is not exceptional; love is.
And judgementalism is not exceptional…but grace is.

Unoffendable

HOPE FROM A PRISON WALL AND A POEM

A California prison wall. Not exactly a place you'd expect to find the words of an 11th century Jewish poem. Yet somehow those words found their way to the third stanza of the old but treasured song: *The Love of God.*

May these words fill your heart and warm your soul today.

"Could we with ink the ocean fill
And were the skies of parchment made;
Were every tree on earth a quill
And every man a scribe by trade;
To write the love of God above
Would drain the ocean dry,
Nor could the scroll contain the whole,
Though stretched from sky to sky.

Oh love of God, how rich and pure!
How measureless and strong!
It shall forevermore endure—
The saints' and angels' song."

The Love of God
Frederick Lehman
(1919)

Hymnary.com is my primary research website for lyrics, author biography, and history of sacred music.

DON'T FENCE ME IN

One morning I awoke with the song *Don't Fence Me In* going over and over in my mind.

This classic song was written in 1934 by Cole Porter and Robert Fletcher and recorded by many people including Roy Rogers. Porter bought a cowboy poem for $250 and made a fortune for himself and others.

Let us take the message of this song to heart today. Whatever comes our way—it will not "fence us in." We will break through and take fresh territory for God—and for us! Look around and break the fence!

Who knows what may be in us that will bless us, our families, and others in the future.

Every time I think of you—and I think of you often—I thank God for your lives of free and open access to God, given by Jesus. There's no end to what has happened in you—it's beyond speech, beyond knowledge. The evidence of Christ has been clearly verified in your lives. 1 Corinthians 1:4-7 MSG.

https://en.wikipedia.org/wiki/Don%27t_Fence_Me_In_(song)

You may be interested in this movie clip featuring Roy Rogers and Trigger performing *Don't Fence Me In.* In today's computerized world with AI generated special effects, Roy and Trigger do some amazing feats in this short film.

https://www.youtube.com/watch?v=kg_zurRBHlg

ONE WORD

On Christmas Eve, 1910, ministers from the Salvation Army met for their annual conference.

Their founder, General William Booth, was severely ill and unable to attend. An advisor suggested he send a telegram to encourage the troops.

Struggling to find the right words to express his faith and to challenge the Army's work, Booth ended up sending a one-word telegram:

"Others"
Signed: General Booth

Be humble, thinking of others as better than yourselves. Don't look out only for your own interests, but take an interest in others, too. You must have the same attitude that Christ Jesus had.
Philippians 2:3-5 NLT

https://www.salvationarmysouthernnevada.org/about-the-salvation-army

1976 CADILLAC COUPE DE VILLE AND A GIANT STUFFED BEAR

As I was accompanying an associate to the Grand Rapids, Michigan Costco, I noticed a beautiful 1976 Cadillac Coupe De Ville parked in the disabled parking section. Given my love for cars, I had to check it out. I asked my host to wait for a few minutes.

The 1976 Coupe De Ville is unusual by today's standards. It was 19 feet long and almost 7 feet wide!

I approached the car and its owner with a friendly wave. Introducing myself, I told him of my love for old cars—and how beautiful his car was. We talked about the car for a few minutes.

In the back seat of this car was a giant stuffed bear. Giant is an appropriate term as its height was from the bench seat to the roof. A rather unusual decoration. I ignored it at first—then I had to ask: "Who is your companion?"

The man told me how the stuffed animal helped him stay sober. He told me his story of a lengthy abuse of alcohol and cigarettes. He never liked to drink alone. So, when he has the urge for a drink, he asks his traveling companion if he wants a drink. The answer is always the same: silence.

Whatever his method, it must be working as he has been sober for 9 years!

I have always believed that when we see something unusual, God is trying to get our attention to teach us something. In this case: a unique car, and unusual decoration led me to a conversation about life and overcoming challenges. I told him how proud I was of him and said, "God is cleaning you up, my friend. He wants to use you." Both of us had the best time; we shook hands and went about our business.

Do not let the unusual stop you.
Watch for it.
Yearn for it.
Learn from it.

...Launch out into the deep.
Luke 5:4 KJV

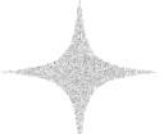

I WILL OUT-SMILE THEM

While lunching with one of my spiritual sons at Chick-fil-A…

Upon completion of my order, I said to the cashier, "I hope everyone is nice to you today!"

The cashier thanked me and said, "If not, I will *out-smile* them … and pray for them!"

Great advice from someone who works with the public. Perhaps we should follow this advice to *out-smile* those who are rude to us … and pray for them!

FILLED WITH LAUGHTER

Behold, God will not reject a man of integrity, nor will He strengthen or support evildoers. He will yet fill your mouth with laughter and your lips with joyful shouting if you are found blameless. Those who hate you will be clothed with shame, and the tents of the wicked will be no longer.

Job 8:20-22 AMP

AT THE INTERSECTION OF ME!

I was running an errand which required me to drive to a part of town with which I was unfamiliar. My GPS was not much help. In frustration, I drove to a parking lot to try to locate where I was in relationship to where I needed to be.

Praying, I asked "God, where am I?" I looked up and I was at the corner of "Thomas Avenue" and "Harrison Street." No joke!

The good news is that I did find my way that morning, yet since that time I've pondered the meaning of that circumstance. Much later I came across this verse of scripture:

I will give you treasures from dark, secret places;
then you will know that I am the LORD and that
the God of Israel has called you by name.
Isaiah 45:3 GNT

Yes, it's relatively unknown. Isaiah is speaking of Cyrus, an ungodly man. Yet God called him by name and used him for His purposes, that of making it possible for the children of Israel to return to the promised land and rebuild the temple. If that was true and it surely was, how much more will God call us, those who have believed upon the name of His Son, Jesus for our salvation!

When we feel lost, how often does the Maker of Heaven and Earth gently remind us that He knows just where we are. Okay, maybe not in this particular manner but in a way that's oh so personal to us.

My friend, He has called you by name and He knows where you are. Reach out to Him in faith today!

OBSERVATIONS FOR A LIFE WELL LIVED

Wherever you go, leave it better than you found it.

Bless everyone with whom you interact.

Focus on others before thinking of yourself.

Earn the right to speak.

Maintain eye contact when you speak to one or to one million. (In person or through Zoom®)

The best gift is to give what is within us … our time … our wisdom … our very selves … and then our resources.

Give more than you take.

Always include the loner, the friendless and those without a champion.

Everyone needs a trusted friend. Batman has Robin, the Lone Ranger has Tonto, the Green Hornet has Kato. Who is your #2?

The older should teach the younger and they can learn … if they're wise enough. The older can learn from the younger … if they're wise enough to listen.

Write thank you notes! They express gratitude and are a rare treasure in our digital world.

Share what you have.

Share what you know.

Now we who are strong ought to bear the weaknesses of those without strength, and not just please ourselves.

Romans 15:1 NASB

GOD KNOWS

**"And I said to the man who stood at the gate of the year:
Give me a light that I may tread safely into the unknown."**

**And he replied:
"Go out into the darkness and put your hand
into the Hand of God.That shall be to you better than
light and safer than a known way."**

The Gate of the Year
originally titled *God Knows*
Minnie Louise Haskins
(1908)

ADOLESCENT REGRET RESOLVED

As a teenager I vividly remember my father telling me that our small family would soon have another member. My brother and I were excited at the possibility of another sibling. While I do not remember what my brother's preference was; I *definitely* wanted a brother. In fact, my parents had not agreed on a name for the new child; and gave my brother and I the privilege of selecting one. "James. We will call him James" I proclaimed in bold adolescent confidence.

I selected the name based on an older friend who had mentored me. It was a regal name, and our parents agreed. To my knowledge, we never discussed a girl's name.

My brother and I were both born on a Friday and in February, but one cold Friday in January, a princess came to live in our home. While I was thankful for a healthy sibling, I was not happy about a sister. In fact, I was disappointed. My plans for a brother were crushed.

This new arrival would likely not enjoy playing in the creek near our home or working with my father in the family business repairing cars. So much for my plans of someone to help grow into a man and follow the family line.

My plans of denim, khakis, and neckties were replaced with bows, ruffles, and hair bands. Outside of my mother, there was no member of our family who changed and laundered more diapers than me. This charming girl had our family's full attention. As my sister grew up,

I would take her with me as I ran errands; little by little this girl-child won my heart, and I became my sister's most ardent and devoted servant and protector.

As often occurs in the course of life, I left our home to attend college and a career hundreds of miles away from the family home. My mother would take my sister to tap dance, ballet and music lessons.

It is interesting how God takes what may have been a disappointment in our life and turns it into something which radically and wondrously blesses us beyond anything we could ask or imagine.

In adulthood my sister helped our family navigate life's troubled seas. She remained steadfast and often immoveable, addressing each of our family's challenges with courage and strength.

If you have ever prayed for a brother and received a sister; I know how you feel. The pain and disillusionment are actually nothing more than adolescent regret. The mature believer knows that we trust God who knows all things and does all things well. My faith is not hindered because I prayed for "X" and received "Y." Rather, I believe God honors all prayers; however, sometimes the answer is "No" or "Wait." Other times, the answer is: "My Son, My Daughter, if you knew what I know, you would have asked for just what I'm getting ready to give you!"

Please do not hold anger and resentment against God (or others) when your prayers are not answered as you requested. God loves us too much to allow hurt and disappointment in our life.

The people were utterly astonished and said,
"He has done all things well!...
Mark 7:37 BSB

SERMONS WE SEE

"I'd rather see a sermon than hear one any day;
I'd rather one should walk with me than merely tell the way.
The eye's a better pupil and more willing than the ear,
Fine counsel is confusing, but example's always clear;
And the best of all the preachers are men who live their creeds,
For to see good put in action is what everybody needs."

Sermons We See
The Light of Faith
© 1926 Edgar A. Guest

During his lifetime, Edgar A. Guest (1881-1959) wrote more than 11,000 poems. His philosophy of writing his poems for newspaper, radio, and television was simple: "I take simple everyday things that happen to me and I figure it happens to a lot of other people, and I make simple rhymes out of them."

There is great power in an illustrated sermon. For years I used episodes of the *Andy Griffith Show* to teach a Sunday School class Biblical truths. I have distributed plastic spoons to illustrate my sermon on 2 Timothy 1:6. (Stir up the gift of God which is in you through the laying on of my hands. NKJV)

We deliver a sermon every day in our community by the way we live.

Conversely, some can become the example of what should *not* be done. *https://poets.org/poet/edgar-guest*

THE VOW OF SILENCE

Once there was a man who had an encounter with God. Not having a church background, the man decided he should visit the local monastery and live among the monks.

Upon arrival he presented himself to the abbot, who informed the man he must obey the vow of silence which the monastic order followed.

At the man's first-year anniversary, he was allowed to say two words. "Think carefully before you speak," cautioned the abbot.

"Food bad." said the man.

On the second anniversary, the man was again allowed to speak two words. "Think carefully before you speak," the abbot reminded him.

"Bed hard." said the man.

After living and working with the monastic order for three years, the man appeared before the abbot and said, "I quit."

The abbot replied: "It's no wonder! All you have done is complain since you arrived."

For the sake of six words spoken during three years, this man was labeled as a complainer.

Perhaps your mother told you: "If you can't say something nice, don't speak."

Death and life are in the power of the tongue,
and those who love it and indulge it will eat its fruit
and bear the consequences of their words.

Proverbs 8:21 AMP

KEEP YOUR BRAIN CELLS!

Noah, a new friend, is working to earn money to begin college. One of Noah's jobs is as a substitute umpire for youth baseball games.

I asked Noah if people ever disagreed with his calls. He answered "All the time. Parents mostly."

Intrigued, I asked him to tell me his most memorable encounter.

It seems the father of one of the players disagreed with a call, then loudly expressed his disagreement to Noah face-to-face.

Good-natured Noah responds, "Dude, I am literally making $20 to umpire this game. Back off."

When we give someone "a piece of our mind" (in reference to complaining) that is exactly what happens—our brain shrinks!

"Research from Stanford University reveals that long-term exposure to stress, such as negativity, actually shrinks the hippocampus in our brain which is responsible for memory, learning and emotions." (Christine Louise Holbaum, Psychology Today, March 11, 2021)

I reminded executives of a Christian organization
that gossip and grumbling among our spiritual ancestors
turned an eleven-day journey into forty years
of wandering in the desert.
Deuteronomy 1:2 AMP

Let all bitterness and wrath and anger and clamor (perpetual animosity, resentment, strife, fault-finding) and slander be put away from you, along with every kind of malice (all spitefulness, verbal abuse, malevolence).
Ephesians 4:31 AMP

The next time we are tempted to give someone a piece of our mind, we should consider whether or not we truly have an abundance of brain cells. Most likely, we need to restrain our temperament and keep our brain cells firmly in place.

PEOPLE-WORK IS MORE IMPORTANT THAN PAPERWORK

"Treat the patient, not the labs" is a wise admonition to first year medical students. While laboratory results are important to diagnose illness, more importantly it is the patient who needs attention.

When my friend, Kirk Hansen, was basketball coach for Central Bible College, he reminded his players: "Watch the game not the scoreboard." Hansen knows basketball. His teams won three national championships, twenty-three regional championships and attained a record of 733-418 in his career. He is a member of the Missouri Sports Hall of Fame and maintains the record as the second-most winning coach in four-year colleges and universities.

In churches or business, we can become so focused on reports and lead measures, we forget the congregation or customers.

Attendance, offerings, customer count, sales, margins, return-on-investment are all measures which we can study; it is the church member or customer that matter.

My son-in-the-faith, Nick Rogers says, "People-work is more important than paperwork."

Nick knows something about both. His portfolio includes the oversight of Roaring Springs Camp and the Christian education experiences for the vast West Texas District. A challenge daunting enough as it stands, however when an August 18, 2024 pop-up storm decimated the camp's Lakeside 300 building, Nick became construction superintendent with few resources to work with apart from the kindness of friends and associates.

Ceilings, walls, furnishings, and infrastructure (plumbing, electrical) all had to be replaced before campers returned. While reconstruction is on-going, Roaring Springs Camp opened this year and hosted numerous camps and receptions serving one thousand students.

When our spiritual ancestor, Nehemiah,
rebuilt the wall in Jerusalem, his resources were limited as well.
Despite opposition and a lack of guaranteed funds,
Nehemiah moved forward and boldly stated "…
the God of Heaven, He will prosper us; therefore we
His servants will arise and build…"
Nehemiah 1:3 KJV

Once the wall was completed, scripture records the
reaction of people far and near. "Now it happened that
when all our enemies heard of it, and all the nations surrounding
us saw it, their confidence fell. And they knew that it was
from our God that this work had been accomplished."
Nehemiah 6:16 LSB

Whatever your challenge in your life, family, church, business, or school, remember it is focusing on the needs of others which brings success.

Now I am giving you a new commandment: Love each other.
Just as I have loved you, you should love each other.
John 13:34 NLT

You may discover more information about West Texas District Next Generation Ministries and Roaring Springs Camp & Retreat Center by visiting **www.wtxnext.com**

Photos by Nick Rogers

COMPLETE YOUR ASSIGNMENT

Despite my occasional losses, I am still a blessed man.

Most of the world walks everywhere; I have three cars but can only drive one at a time.

Most of the world sleeps outdoors or in substandard housing; I have a house with heat and air conditioning, indoor plumbing, and modern conveniences.

Most of the world eats rice and drinks water if they have food; I have a variety of food in my refrigerator and pantry and I can purchase food at any hour in abundance at a nearby grocery store or restaurant.

Good things happen to bad people and good people.

Bad things happen to bad people and good people.

Health challenges, job losses, economic disasters, and family problems do not discriminate. In this regard the children of God, and I certainly profess to be one, are not unlike those without faith in Him.

The Christian understands that it is God who provides and protects.

Cast your burden on the LORD, and He will sustain you;
He will never permit the righteous to be moved.
Psalm 55:22 ESV

Those who look to Him for help will be radiant with joy;
no shadow of shame will darken their faces.
Psalm 34:5 NLT

My friend, whatever may come your way during this season of life, know that God still desires you to complete your assigned work.

Though I walk in the midst of trouble, you preserve my life;
you stretch out your hand against the wrath of my enemies,
and your right hand delivers me. The Lord will fulfill his
purpose for me; your steadfast love, O Lord, endures forever.
Do not forsake the work of your hands.
Psalm 138:7-8 ESV

INSPIRATIONAL QUOTATIONS (I WISH I HAD SAID)

"Almost everything will work again if you unplug it for a few minutes, including you."

Anne Lamott

"Life's toughest battles are fought and won in your mind, so the Devil will attack your thoughts. Are you winning or losing the battle?"

Rodney Hutcheson

"You can contribute nothing to your salvation except the sin that made it necessary."

Attributed to

Jonathan Edwards

"A mentor is someone whose hindsight can be your foresight."

Fortune Cookie

"Anything of consequence starts with...one.
One prayer. One step. One brick. One act. One move.
Ask God for the courage to set in motion something new today."

Nick Rogers

"Be kinder than necessary."

David Ingles

"Waiting is one of the hardest things the Lord ever asks us to do but it always works for our good. Stay strong my friend."

Richard Exley

"Bitterness can turn you into the person who hurt you."

T.F. Tenney

"God gave us a brain to use. If we do not use it, whose fault is that?"

Mary Harrison

(The author's mother)

"Champions do not become champions when they win the event, but in the hours, weeks, months, and years they spend preparing for it. The victorious performance itself is merely the demonstration of their championship character."

Alan Armstrong

"God is looking for wicks to burn; the oil and the fire are free."

Hudson Taylor

"Stop articulating your victimhood and start declaring your victory in Christ."

Eric Smith

"Honor is the destination of every man.

Honor is the vehicle that takes him to his destination, and it is ethics that he holds. What sustains him in the midst of the turbulent journey is his integrity. When people see your ethics as you keep your word, they in turn will give you honor."

Jerry Edmon

"I've got my faults but living in the past is not one of them. There's no future in it."

Sparky Anderson

"Surround yourself with people who believe in you more than you do in yourself."

Gaby Natale

"If you don't ask, the answer is always "No."

Kathy Harrison

(The author's wife)

"The chains of habit are too light to be felt until they are too heavy to be broken."

Samuel Johnson

"There are far better things ahead than any we leave behind."

C. S. Lewis

"The resurrection of Jesus is a historical fact,
a present reality and our future hope!"

Richard Exley

"Unfortunately, there seems to be far more opportunity out there than ability…We should remember that good fortune often happens when opportunity meets with preparation."

Thomas A. Edison

"When the manager enjoys their job,
the employees tend to be happier."

Josh Swarer

(The author's nephew)

"Who does not thank for little will not thank for much."

Estonian Proverb

"You are never too old to reinvent yourself."

Steve Harvey

NOT ONLY IN HIS SUFFERINGS

All who follow the leading of God's Sprit are God's own sons. Nor are you meant to relapse into the old slavish attitude of fear—you have been adopted into the very family circle of God and you can say with a full heart, "Father, my Father". The Spirit himself endorses our inward conviction that we really are the children of God. Think what that means. If we are his children we share his treasures, and all that Christ claims as his will belong to all of us as well! Yes, if we share in his suffering we shall certainly share in his glory.

Romans 8:14-17 Phillips

LOVE PAID THE RANSOM FOR ME

Tell of the cross where they nailed Him,
Writhing in anguish and pain;
Tell of the grave where they laid Him,
Tell how He liveth again.
Love in that story so tender,
Clearer than ever I see:
Stay, let me weep while you whisper,
Love paid the ransom for me.

Tell me the story of Jesus,
Write on my heart every word;
Tell me the story most precious,
Sweetest that ever was heard.

Tell Me The Story of Jesus
Fanny Crosby
(1880)

This verse was on my mind as I awoke this morning.
Let us never forget: "Love paid the ransom for me!"

For the Son of Man came not to be served,
but to serve, and to give his life a ransom for many.
Mark 10:45 NRSV

Hymnary.org is my primary research website for lyrics, author biography, and history of sacred music.

THE DAY A TRUCK STOP BECAME A CATHEDRAL OF PRAYER

An account of one man's decades of generosity intrigued me. It seemed everywhere I traveled, this man's beneficence was told and retold.

During times of famine and economic downturn, one farmer dedicated his life and crops to the glory of God. Existence at times was barely enough to feed his family, let alone provide produce for others. It was at a revival meeting when a certain farmer made a decision to believe God to bless not only his crops but those of his neighbors. He began bringing produce to the church to bless the pastor and the evangelist. Then the farmer encouraged other farmers to bless the church with *their* crops.

This began a revival not only in the church but in the fields. One by one, farmers experienced a bountiful supply. A year or so later in successive revivals with the same evangelist, the farmer encouraged his neighbors to believe God that they could send a railroad car full of produce for a missions project.

This man was so blessed by God that for almost fifty years, he supplied produce by the truckload to a mission.

If such a legend were true, I had to meet the man who had believed God to feed an entire mission for fifty years.

When I discovered a new friend knew this man's pastor, I called the pastor who was also known for his generosity. I asked if I could meet his legendary congregant. A few minutes later, a meeting was set—at a truck stop. I drove 700 miles round trip to meet this man who had served, at least for me, almost like the definition of giving.

Our lunch meeting at the truck stop was grand. Three men met as strangers yet a few minutes into the meeting we seemed as old friends.

I had an idea how the meeting would go—but my idea was superseded by God's plan.

The legendary farmer told how he had been blessed by God many times and from all accounts he *was* blessed. Then he told of heartache and in tears asked for prayer.

"Could we pray now?!" I asked.

At a window table at a truck stop, we had a prayer meeting.

This man was accustomed to people asking him for finances or products. That day, I offered prayer and encouraging words.

Friends, sometimes people — no matter who they are and no matter what they have accomplished during their lives — just need us to listen. They need to know we care.

Do not allow someone's social or financial status to intimidate you.

...Be instant in season and out of season...
2 Timothy 4:2 KJV

MY FAITH HAS FOUND A RESTING PLACE

My faith has found a resting place,
Not in device or creed;
I trust the ever-living One,
His wounds for me shall plead.

I need no other argument,
I need no other plea,
It is enough that Jesus died,
And that He died for me.

My Faith Has Found A Resting Place
E. E. Hewitt (1881)

The old songs teach a body of principles found in scripture. It is amazing that after all these years, this hymn is still teaching us that all we need is Jesus.

Hymnary.org is my primary research website for lyrics, author biography, and history of sacred music.

MY ENCOUNTER WITH A CELEBRITY WHO TREATED ME LIKE A PRINCE

In the 1990's, I was invited to serve as the Master of Ceremonies for a fundraising banquet benefiting John 3:16 Mission in Tulsa, Oklahoma. It was a dream come true assignment, as I have admired the work of John 3:16 for years.

Offering the invocation and praying for the meal that evening was Tulsa pastor, Dr. Warren Hultgren.

Before the banquet began, I noticed Dr. Hultgren sitting in the hotel lobby ... alone. I greeted Dr. Hultgren and introduced myself.

Dr. Hultgren was no stranger to these activities; he pastored First Baptist Church in Tulsa from 1957 to 1992—35 years. (You can only imagine how many fried chicken dinners he has prayed over!)

Dr. Hultgren said to me: "Let me ask you a question, young man. If you were giving the invocation and praying for the meal tonight, what would you do?" I politely responded with a few thoughts, but clearly, he had this.

That night, one of the most respected men of faith in Tulsa—if not Oklahoma or the world—asked my opinion. He did not recite his resume to me, nor tell me of his close associations with Dr. Billy Graham and Evangelist Oral Roberts—nor of the influential people who attended his church. He asked a skinny young *kid*— "What would you do if you were me?"

How we could infuse confidence in the lives of others by asking, "What would you do if you were me?"

Do nothing from selfish ambition or conceit,
but in humility count others more significant than yourselves.
Philippians 2:3 ESV

Agree with each other, love each other, and be deep-spirited friends. Don't push your way to the front; don't sweet-talk your way to the top. Put yourself aside, and help others get ahead.
Philippians 2: 2-3 MSG

If you want to know more about this man, check out the articles below. The Tulsa World wrote a story about the legacy of Dr. Hultgren—10 years after his death!

Dr. Hultgren Obituary

https://tulsaworld.com/news/local/longtime-tulsa-baptist-minister-warren-hultgren-dies-at-89/article_dc0581be-16c7-57ae-9ad5-cc9c6e8756a9.html

Dr. Hultgren Tribute—10 years after his death

https://tulsaworld.com/news/local/michael-overall-tulsas-pastor-still-getting-praise-a-decade-after-his-death/article_bd5a2522-3646-11eb-b514-8792c0e0e4d9.html

SLEEPING IN CHURCH?

While I was Interim Pastor of a church in Northeastern Oklahoma, my goal was to keep the church moving forward while they searched for a Senior Pastor. It was an excellent assignment, and I learned much during my months with the congregation.

One Sunday morning, I mentioned from the pulpit: "If you sleep in church, that does not bother me! I have been known to nod off on occasion in church. Think about it. We sleep because we are not fearful of what may happen—we are safe. We sleep because we are comfortable, in a setting with people we know, listening to music we like. Many have strenuous jobs, and Sunday is perhaps your only time to rest. I would rather you come to church and sleep than stay home and sleep."

My observations about sleeping in church lasted three minutes.

After the service, I would greet as many people as possible. While shaking hands, I noticed a couple waiting to speak to me. Making my way to where they were, I greeted the couple.

"This is our first time here, and we want to ask you a question. Did you mean what you said about sleeping in church?"

I replied: "Yes, every word!"

"My husband sleeps in church and has for years. He feels terrible about it, and there is nothing he can do to stop it. We have been to several churches, and they do not understand. This is the first time we have heard a minister say he would be welcomed if he slept in church."

My heart sank when I realized the guilt this man has carried for years.

I told the man (who had not said a word to this point) that I understood. He smiled in agreement.

The man was a retired executive with a major petroleum company, and they continued to attend every service.

The guilt people carry about with them can be overwhelming and crippling. I made what I thought was a casual comment; however, the Holy Spirit knew what that man needed to be set free from guilt.

Speak words of health, healing, and deliverance.

Nevertheless, I will bring health and healing to it;
I will heal my people and will let them enjoy
abundant peace and security.
Jeremiah 33:6 ESV

OH COME, OH COME, EMMANUEL

Oh come, Oh come, Emmanuel
And ransom captive Israel
That mourns in lonely exile here
Until the Son of God appear

Oh come, Thou Wisdom from on high
and order all things far and nigh
To us the path of knowledge show
And cause us in her ways to go

Rejoice! Rejoice! Emmanuel
Shall come to thee O Israel

Oh Come, Oh Come, Emmanuel
John Mason Neale
(Translated 1844)

We, like that inn keeper of old, may not have room in the inn of our hearts for Jesus.

May our hearts be open and receptive as the lowly stable to receive the gift of Jesus.

Hymnary.org is my primary research website for lyrics, author biography, and history of sacred music.

ENCOURAGING WORDS

The right word at the right time is like precious gold set in silver.
Proverbs 25:11 CEB

Generously speak encouraging words today.
You may prevent a heart from breaking.

Photo by Tim Maroney

SQUEEZED BUT NOT STRANGLED!

The Christian is not immune from problems, trials of life, or setbacks.

Beloved, do not be surprised at the fiery ordeal which is taking place to test you (that is, to test the quality of your faith), as though something strange or unusual were happening to you.
1 Peter 4:12 AMP

When these events come our way, we can act or react. We can react by proclaiming the problem or we can act by taking a positive outlook, exercising spiritual authority.

While God does not send destruction and lack, He can use these circumstances to develop our faith and trust in Him.

And we know (with great confidence) that God (who is deeply concerned about us) causes all things to work together (as a plan) for good for those who love God, to those who are called according to His plan and purpose.
Romans 8:28 AMP

Whatever you are facing, remind yourself that God will not harm you. Rather, He will use this season to build you.

For we are squeezed in all things, but we are not strangled; we are harassed, but we are not condemned. We are persecuted, but we are not forsaken; We are cast down, but we are not defeated.
2 Corinthians 4:8-9 ABPE

Keep praising God and proclaiming the goodness of God.

Many adversities come to the one who is righteous, but the LORD delivers him from them all.
Psalm 34:19 HCS

God has a history of delivering His people during times of oppression. He sees you. He will deliver you.

SHUT IN WITH GOD

Shut in with God
in a secret place;
There in the Spirit
beholding His face;
Gaining more power
to run in the race,
I love to be
shut in with God.

Shut In With God
William Grum (1940)

Former Superintendent for the Oklahoma Assemblies of God, Armon Newburn sang this song often. May we be shut in with God as we find new power through the Holy Spirit.

My friend, may God bless you in so many ways you will need an abacus (or perhaps an instrument much more sophisticated) to count them!

Humnary.org is my primary research website for lyrics, author biography, and history of sacred music.

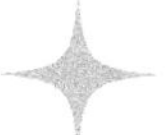

WHEN ALL THAT REMAINS IS AN EMPTY BOX

Moreno was a young man living in Spain who craved adventure, so he became a bullfighter.

At the age of 15, Moreno was seriously injured in a bullfighting accident. Doctors urged him to exercise his injured arm, so he began juggling.

Always the class clown, he loved to make people laugh.

Moreno traveled with a circus juggling, spinning plates, and performing with puppets he handcrafted.

In 1936, a train accident demolished his puppets … so … he improvised using vocal tricks and an empty box to create the illusion of someone living in the box talking to him. His main puppet, "Johnny," was actually Moreno's hand decked out with makeup, wig, and costume.

You may not recognize the name Wenceslco Moreno, but millions around the world found humor in the character Señor Wences, the noted ventriloquist.

An otherwise average man, Moreno had more setbacks than one usually encounters in life.

He was a guest on *The Ed Sullivan Show* a record 48 times. Sullivan never pronounced his name correctly, yet Moreno was not offended when the host had so much trouble saying his name. Moreno would simply re-introduce himself as he began his act. (Problem solved.)

Before he died, Moreno gave his puppets to a fellow ventriloquist who uses them and some original material in a new act for new audiences.

Do we want to be known for our injuries and scars or reach for the stars?

When our world crashes, we can find new avenues by using what remains—even an empty box. We can make our formerly injured hand a puppet.

Shall we count our losses or treasure our assets?

Focus on what remains.

God asked Moses, "What is in your hand?"
Exodus 4:2 NASB

The next time the train wreck of life ruins your plans, be thankful for the empty box which remains.

https://en.wikipedia.org/wiki/Se%C3%B1or_Wences

Perhaps you would enjoy this video clip of our friend, Moreno.
https://youtu.be/SLHEPTfshCI

SNOW BY THE TRUCKLOADS

My career as a Secret Church Shopper has been rewarding and has taken me across the country from California to New York. What's a Secret Church Shopper, you might ask? Churches of all sizes and denominations have requested my services over the years to quietly observe any number of things about the church — problems the pastoral leadership may not have noticed, things obvious to the congregation perhaps which are causing the church to even lose membership and the like. Such issues can be found all the way from the pulpit to the vestibule to the choir, to perhaps unfriendly greeters or even to the restrooms. My work has been featured in the *Wall Street Journal*, CBN's *700 Club*, *Tulsa World*, *The Oklahoman*, *Oasis Radio Network*, *LeSEA Network*, *Daystar Network*, and scores of other publications and media outlets.

I could tell you multiple stories of my adventures and findings. One practice has been never to reveal the identity of a client church or organization.

In mid-December 2009, I flew to Orange County, California, to help a church.

Arriving a few days early to enjoy the sun and beach, it was a rather stark contrast to Christmas in the Midwest and South.

Imagine my surprise as I arrive at the church and the common areas are covered with *snow*.

Real, cold, wet snow!

This church regularly imports snow by truckload for a massive community outreach each Christmas season.

Snow slides, snowball fights, and building snowmen are among the activities.

I was in total disbelief and speechless.

Some of the children in that neighborhood have only known snow from television shows, movies, or books.

It wasn't spiritual, but it was a kind thing to do. It helped bring out the child in the workers and one secret guest from the Midwest.

Relating this story to a minister friend, "I'm struggling to find a spiritual lesson or context." Then I remembered this verse:

Like the cold of snow (brought from the mountains) in the time of harvest, So is a faithful messenger to those who send him; For he refreshes the life of his masters.
Proverbs 25:13 AMP

What a lovely thing for this church to do for all who attended. How refreshing! And the refreshment trickled down from "the masters" to all who had eyes to see.

Is there room in our faith to bless people in unusual and extravagant ways?

I would say a fervent and excited YES!

JESUS IS COMING SOON

"Troublesome times are here, filling men's hearts with fear. Freedom we all hold dear now is at stake. Humbling your hearts to God, saves from the chastening rod. Seek the way pilgrims trod. Christians awake!

Jesus is coming soon, morning or night or noon.
Many will meet their doom, trumpets will sound.
All of the dead shall rise, righteous meet in the skies.
Going where no one dies, heavenward bound."

Jesus Is Coming Soon
© 1942 R. E. Winsett

No matter what happens; one thing on which we can rely is that Jesus is coming soon!

The news may be depressing, and we may feel downtrodden. Rest assured our Father cares for you! Your work is important!

Jesus is coming, soon!

Hymnary.org is my primary research website for lyrics, author biography, and history of sacred music.

"THAT'S GOD..."

I met a young man a few weeks ago who told me he believed God was changing his direction. He was unsettled and unsure how to move forward. Each time I saw him, I spoke affirming words of encouragement.

This week when I saw him, he expressed doubt in his abilities. I told him, "Whatever God has for you to do, you are enough." As soon as I said this, his complexion turned red, and he became quiet. I whispered to him, "I did not mean to embarrass you. I am sorry." His response, "I am not embarrassed. As soon as you said that I felt warmth come all over me." I told him, "That is God giving you a hug."

I have often said I am God's cheerleader, cheering His people along, helping them to believe in themselves and in the work God has for them. God gives us specific words by the inspiration of the Holy Spirit....

The one who prophesies speaks to people for edification (to promote their spiritual growth) and (speaks words of) encouragement (to uphold and advise them concerning the matters of God) and (speaks words of) consolation (to compassionately comfort them).

1 Corinthians 14:3 AMP

And let us consider how we may spur one another on toward love and good deeds...
Hebrews 10:24 NIV

With everything that is within me, I want to encourage people to succeed as they advance on their mission for God. I know that is your mission as well.

TAKE TIME FOR YOURSELF

I admit my tendency to take care of others before taking care of myself. It is easy to address the needs of others and forget my own needs.

I should take time to take care of me too. You may have a similar trait. If so, we should reform.

Dr. Dan Beller, former pastor of Evangelistic Temple in Tulsa, Oklahoma told me his secret for recharging his body before going home for the day.

Pastor Beller would drive to a parking lot and take a nap before heading home. This way he could be refreshed for his family.

It worked well and none were the wiser until one day when someone knocked on his window to see if he was "ok." And he was recognized by a parishioner.

In this season of hustle and bustle, text or call a friend, take the dog for a walk, or like Pastor Beller, find a secluded parking spot for a quick recharge.

He refreshes *and* restores my soul (life);
He leads me in the paths of righteousness for His name's sake.
Psalm 23:3 AMP

TAUGHT BY AN OLD DRAFT HORSE

Several years ago, I was the general manager of a television station in Tulsa, Oklahoma. Our owners had several other stations, and we had meetings at different locations where the various other stations were located. This one occurred in Saint Joseph, Missouri (where the Pony Express began, and Jesse James ended.)

One day we had an excursion into the country to ride horses for recreational activity. In my youth I had ridden horses (and even a goat or two) on my grandfather's farm. I thought I knew all I needed to know about riding a trail horse.

My stallion was an old gray draft horse. He was sturdy, and you could tell he had paid his dues working on farms. His life now consisted of taking tourists on trail rides—over and over the same trail—day after day.

A recent rain had made the trail slick in spots, and a few areas were quite muddy. When my horse would go in a direction I did not want to go, I pulled tight on the reins to make a course correction. The horse grudgingly responded. The descent in the trail was muddy, and I pulled tight again. This time the horse reacted differently.

The next thing I knew, my left knee was forced against a tree. That was a life lesson for me. Who was I to tell this horse how to do his job? He obviously knew the trail much better than I did and had wisdom about navigating uncertain obstacles. From that moment until the end of the trail ride, I let the horse guide me on the trail. It was the best part of the experience—letting the horse do his job.

When we allow the Holy Spirit to guide us, our journey in life is directed by the Maker of Heaven and Earth. (Psalm 124:8)

Similarly, when others perform services for us—it is best to let them do their job. We can request our preferences, but trusting the master craftsman is always the better route.

Show me your ways, LORD, teach me your paths.
Psalm 25:4 NIV

THE BLINKING WARNING LIGHT

Camped out in a corner table at Chick-fil-A in Muskogee, Oklahoma, I was in the midst of preparing my sermon for an upcoming ministry opportunity. From the table next to me came a voice interrupting my study:

HIM: "Are you writing a sermon?"

ME: "Yes."

HIM: "Want to try it out on us?" (Actual quote!)

ME: "My name is Thomas."

HIM: "I am D.J. This is my (teenage) son, Christopher."

ME: "Do you live in Muskogee?"

HIM: "We live in Michigan, and we are traveling back home from Texas, and my son is hungry."

ME: (I tell them I am ministering in Norman, Oklahoma the following Sunday. In five minutes, I give them my message, along with scriptures.)

HIM: "That is very good. Thank you." (Teenage son—very mature and polite— agrees.)

ME: "May I pray with you about something?" (Understand, I just met these people a few minutes ago. I am expecting to hear, "We are good.")

HIM: "Yes. We have a blinking warning light on the dashboard in the car." (Teenage son, ever-so-slightly and unseen by his father—rolls his eyes.)

ME: (Knowing they have hundreds of miles to travel and knowing something about cars since childhood—I pray for them at the table for the car's warning light, for their safety, and ask God to protect and bless them.)

HIM: (We talk Oklahoma and Muskogee history —with me telling them I used to pastor here in Muskogee ... we talk famous people from Oklahoma. Thanks me and excuses himself from the table)

ME: (I tell Christopher how much it made my day that they said something.)

HIM: (Returns to the table) "The blinking light is off!"

ME: "May I give you a copy of my book?" (I sign and present the book to them.)

It was a grand encounter.

Ministry is being available for people, ready to listen and providing an encouraging word and prayer.

Be ready to spread the word whether or not the time is right... Warn people, and encourage them. Be very patient when you teach.

2 Timothy 4:2 GWT

Photo by Cory Zollo

INVEST YOUR OWN SELF

As an associate pastor at a large church in the Tulsa, Oklahoma area, my job description included selecting, training, and assigning college interns for our church.

I traveled to a Christian university, conducted interviews, and selected candidates to spend the summer in a paid internship.

I invested in interns providing them education, ministry training and recreation. Often one or more would accompany me on hospital visits, church or district business, even assisting with funeral ministry. I invited interns to my home for meals, recreation, and fellowship.

Years later, one intern, Lee, became a true spiritual son. We have been overnight guests in each other's homes, exchanged ideas by text, telephone calls, emails, and in person. We encouraged each other's pursuit of ministry and higher education. We supported each other during dry seasons and halcyon days. Lee is now Dr. Guidry, an associate professor at his alma mater and doctoral dissertation chair for another university. He continues to honor and bless me.

I have his permission to share the following:

"By the way my meeting with the Chief Academic Officer of the Ministry of Education of Grenada went well. I have an open invitation to bring a team down next March to work with the public school system there.

I used the Thomas Harrison method. He asked what it was we wanted to do. I told him to tell me what we could do that would benefit Grenadian schools and what we need to accomplish would be a natural byproduct of that.

That made him smile and he asked if we could do a STEM (Science, Technology, Engineering, Mathematics) lesson with a school and some teacher Professional Development.

I said "Done!""

Never discount anyone. Encourage everyone.

So, being affectionately desirous of you, we were ready to share with you not only the gospel of God but also our own selves, because you had become very dear to us.
1 Thessalonians 2:8 ESV

PRESERVED

My grandfather preserved (or *saved* as he called it) fruits and vegetables in glass jars and stored them in his cellar on his farm. How wonderful to enjoy those fruits during the off season.

Whosoever shall call upon the name of the
Lord shall be *preserved for future use.*
Harrison's Commentary on
Romans 10:13 KJV

Surely all players prepare for the game, but all players do not play the game at the same time.

We serve at God's command and timing.

ARE YOU DETERMINED?

I am determined to be invincible
'Til He has finished His purpose in me.
And nothing shall shake me
For He'll never forsake me
And I am determined to live for the King.

Hell's gates are trembling from our prayers ascending.
Darkness is crumbling from praises we sing.
Our Sovereign, Victorious is marching before us,
And We are determined to live for the King.

I Am Determined To Live For The King
© 1995 Jennifer LaMountain

I am determined to serve God when I do good, and when I fail. Failure is an event, not a lifestyle.

If you have temporarily stumbled along life's race, ask God for forgiveness. Then forgive yourself and continue the race.

The enemy of our soul would have us living in fear and regret; constantly condemning us for our past mistakes.

If we confess our sins, He is faithful and just and will forgive us our sins and purify us from all unrighteousness.
1 John 1:9 NIV

THE CHURCH'S ONE FOUNDATION
A Resurrection Day Message

The Church's one foundation
Is Jesus Christ her Lord;
She is his new creation,
By water and the word;
From Heav'n he came and sought her
To be his holy bride;
With his own blood he bought her,
And for her life he died.

The Church's One Foundation
S. J. Stone (1866)

If you are a worker in the Lord's church; your work is holy. On this holy day, consider the matchless and sacrificial gift of the Church to the Body of Christ.

On this day, know that the greater one lives in you!

Ye are of God, little children and have overcome them: because greater is he that is in you, than he that is in the world.
1 John 4:4 KJV

Hymnary.com is my official source for lyrics and biographical information on composers.

Photo by Joshua Somma

TEARS ARE A LANGUAGE GOD UNDERSTANDS

My brother and I are 735 days apart in age, five days beyond being exactly two years apart. We are opposites in many ways. Our vocational training and career choices fit our talents, personalities, and natural abilities—except for one. My brother can cry.

Crying is not essential in my brother's profession but he loves people so much that he can cry *on cue*. I have to work up a good cry.

One day in prayer, I told God how unfair this was that my younger brother could cry, but I could not. Then I asked God, "Could I have the gift of crying?"

I don't recall when or how it happened, but a while later, I noticed I began to shed tears. Real tears.

I cried freely and often. I cried when my friends experienced pain, grief, or death. I would cry during the movies or while watching something poignant on television.

There are times when I have been so moved while telling a story or explaining something that tears flowed freely and beyond my control. In those moments, I hear the voice of the Holy Spirit say to me, "This is what you asked for." I have never complained nor regretted my request for the gift of crying.

My father cried only during times of intense emotional stress or unrelenting pain. His generation and those before him were taught to be strong, and tears were not a sign of masculinity.

The first song I heard my wife and her sister sing in church was: *Tears Are A Language God Understands*, written by Gordon Jensen.

My friend, if you are crying, please know your tears are important to God as He saves them in a bottle (Psalm 56:8). Like the Psalmist, tears may be your food day and night (Psalm 42:3). We who cry today will one day laugh (Luke 6;21). It is healthy and human to show emotion and cry.

The gift of crying humbles me. It shows others that something touched my heart and even my soul. I am thankful I asked God for the gift of crying.

Be careful what you ask God for; He may honor your prayers.

I hope he does honor your prayers, well, the wise ones anyway!

THE RAFFLE

While working as Associate Pastor of a large church near Tulsa, Oklahoma I also taught a Sunday School class. This was no ordinary class as I used episodes of *The Andy Griffith Show* to illustrate Biblical themes.

One Sunday we were having an indoor picnic with a raffle. (Mind you, this was just a *drawing* for a prize. No money was exchanged!)

Earlier in the week I secured a quilt from a thrift store. I purposely selected the most bizarre-looking quilt available; a 1970's polyester yarn in multiple colors. My intent was to get the class laughing once the gift was opened.

The appointed time for the raffle arrived. With great fanfare I drew a name... "Nellie, you are our winner—come on down!"

The class cheered and applauded.

Nellie was a quiet, older woman who lived by herself. Often, the church would give her a gift basket for Christmas. She was shy and always blended into a crowd.

Nellie opened the box ... and tears began to roll down her face.

"This is beautiful." Then the words I have never forgotten since. "Pastor Thomas, I have never won anything in my life!"

In an instant, I realized my motive was wrong. While the quilt wasn't my style, it was beautiful in the eyes of a woman who would see it for what it was—a priceless gift from her church who serves the God she loves and follows.

Who taught the lesson that day?

Friends, let us celebrate everyone. Find beauty in the seemingly ugly.

Oh, that we could celebrate when we are given a gift the way Nellie taught the Mayberry class.

Be devoted to one another with mutual love,
showing eagerness in honoring one another.
Romans 12:10 NET

MY CONFIDENCE IS GREAT

Faith comes by hearing the Word
Sweet is the secret I've learned
I'll sow seed, the Spirit heed
And always have plenty
Come what may, I'll always overcome.

My confidence is great in the Lord
Because I believe in God's Word
I'm going forth and doing great exploits
My confidence is great in the Lord.

I'll keep meditating day and night
I'll continue fighting the good fight
I'll observe to do God's Word
And all that's written there
To revelation truth I'll be aware.

My confidence is great in the Lord
Because I believe in God's Word
I'm going forth and doing great exploits
My confidence is great in the Lord.

Knowing we're encompassed about
With many faithful witnesses devout
Hearing cheering from the grandstands
They keep yelling, You can do it!
Makes me want to keep on keeping on.

My Confidence Is Great (In The Lord)
© 2009 David Ingles

Let us therefore come boldly to the throne of grace, that we may obtain mercy and find grace to help in time of need.
Hebrews 4:16 NKJV

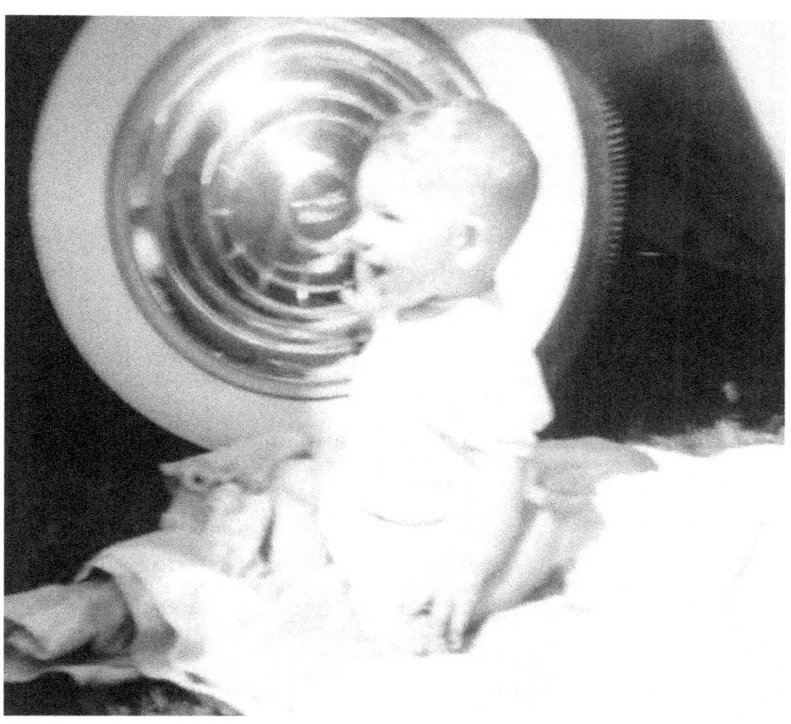

My love for cars began at an early age.

THE FAMILY NAME

A *good* name [earned by honorable behavior, godly wisdom, moral courage, and personal integrity] is more desirable than great riches; And favor is better than silver and gold.
Proverbs 22:1 AMP

My parents, Thomas and Mary Harrison, provided good examples for what the name *Harrison* was to represent during our growing-up years. The name Harrison was to be defined as *service to others.*

The reader will learn in another story in this volume how my father and I came to be named *Thomas.* (See *Life-Giving Water From Two Wounded Ones.*) Dad chose the shorter and colloquial versions which he used interchangeably; I chose the formal.

My father's occupation listed on my birth certificate reads *body and fender man.* After serving in the military, he was employed by various auto repair facilities before starting his own business. His story is featured as *The Strongest Man in Our Neighborhood,* the first story in *Move Up! Don't Give Up!* In repairing cars for his clients, I remember so well the dedication and service to others exhibited by my father.

My mother, after leaving the family farm, attended cosmetology school where she learned how to cut, style, wave, and color hair. Mom worked for several beauty shops before she opened her own salon. She always made herself available to style hair for weddings, social events, and the ladies who would come in every week for a quick style before the weekend. Mom's service included assisting one musical family (a mother and her daughters) who regularly appeared on local television.

The musical family operated a daycare facility, where my younger brother and I attended before elementary school. They produced a Christmas production of the birth of Jesus. Sets and costumes were crafted by the local high school and a studio choir was assembled and led by a neighbor who lived three doors down from our house. The cast consisted entirely of children from the daycare center, including this author who was cast as Joseph and my brother who played a shepherd.

The Christmas program was aired on KARK TV, the local NBC affiliate in Little Rock, Arkansas. That night I fell in love with television — appearing in front of the camera — and I would spend the remainder of my life doing so ... concomitantly acquiring knowledge and academic degrees in media. I remember that night so vividly. As a reward for a job well done, my parents presented me with a large red fire truck.

Little did this family realize the doors they opened, not only for their children but others, to pursue avenues yet unknown to formative minds.

My father added a wrecker service to complement his auto repair facility, beginning with a factory-ordered wrecker from Ernest Holmes Company in Chattanooga, Tennessee. He was, in my estimation, a marketing genius, advertising his services as "23 ½ hour Wrecker Service." I suppose Dad had to sleep, eat a sandwich or a slice of cornbread during his *proverbial* thirty minutes off from work.

Dad would often take food to his employees who had fallen on tough times. As a pre-teenager, I remember going with him on many such occasions; even to bail people out of jail.

Today, my brother operates the business our father began so many years ago. My sister works for a company that provides employers with payroll services. Each of us continues the value of *service to others* which our parents demonstrated right before our eyes.

There was another family who *inadvertently* influenced me and while I have never written about them, I have spoken about how another *Thomas Harrison* influenced my life.

As I began my personal and professional journey working in full-time Christian service at churches, Christian radio and television stations, and educational institutions, I introduced myself as "Thomas Harrison." I was often asked if I were related to *the* Thomas Harrison who was a college professor. Not knowing of this man, I would answer in the negative.

When working with the Assemblies of God, the *other* Thomas Harrison's name would surface. While I knew there could be no relation, I always asked those people who knew him to tell me a story about him. One pastor showed me his briefcase with considerable pride declaring, "He was my favorite Bible professor. I bought this briefcase because he carried one just like it!" Others described more personal stories of how Dr. Thomas Franklin Harrison had assisted them.

Dr. Thomas F. Harrison was an Assemblies of God minister, ordained in 1948 at the age of nineteen. He and Louise K. Harrison served churches, Bible colleges and the Assemblies of God as a movement. Dr. Harrison later served as the Chairman of the Christian Biblical Education Division at Central Bible College. He authored several publications including two textbooks, *Christology* (1985) and *Soteriology* (1986).

Dr. Thomas F. Harrison and I are not related, except through the blood of Jesus, yet in addition to our names, the similarities are numerous. We both were/are pastors, ministers and served/serve the Assemblies of God. Central Bible College employed both of us, although he as chairman and me as adjunct professor. We are both (were/are) authors, and our wives were/are educators. While we never met, his last home in the town where I now live is less than three miles from mine.

While I would never claim to be in any way equal to this man, his name has opened countless doors for me.

A most humorous story about the *other* Thomas Harrison occurred on the evening of my ordination into the ministry in Oklahoma City, Oklahoma. At the conclusion of the ordination ceremony, the ordination candidates and spouses were called to the altar area for prayer and the laying on of hands. (Hebrews 6:2) A protracted line of pastors, officials, and friends came to extend their congratulations.

Two elderly women came and remarked at my last name, with the suffix "Jr." In unison they said: "Oh, we knew your dad. You look just like him!" (Of course they were referring to the *other* Thomas Harrison.) My wife, Kathy, standing near, and always the diplomat, responded: "Yes. He does look just like his father."

Through the years, I have collected stories about Dr. Thomas F. Harrison. His personal library was donated to what is now Nelson University in Waxahachie, Texas who named its library in his honor. Throughout the years, I enjoyed touring the campus. I was there on official business one day when I introduced myself to a student worker and asked for directions. Her reply, "*The* Thomas Harrison, like the library, Thomas Harrison?" My response, "I am *a* Thomas Harrison, not *the* Thomas Harrison."

Dear Reader, how many good names contributed to just this portion of my story? Our family name, the musical family's name (and the daycare they operated), the television station's good name, Ernest Holmes Company, Nelson University, and of course Dr. Thomas F. Harrison. It's so easy to forget all the seemingly small things which worked together to formulate who we are.

The steps of a good man are ordered by the LORD,
And He delights in his way.
Psalm 37:23 NKJV

How many good names have contributed to *your* story and to *your* success? It is doubtful you could number them all if you tried — what on the surface are casual occurrences that turned into lifelong careers.

Better still, how many will say *your* good name has helped *them* to succeed?

I hope I have lived a life that made both Thomas Harrisons pleased with my actions, conduct, and accomplishments.

THE GENEROSITY FACTOR

While attending a conference I had the opportunity to meet management guru Ken Blanchard, co-author of *The One Minute Manager*. I read the book years ago, a phenomenal success selling 15 million copies.

Blanchard co-authored a book with S. Truett Cathy (founder of Chick-fil-A), *The Generosity Factor*. The conference was giving away copies of *The Generosity Factor.*

Blanchard inscribed a copy to me; I thanked him and went on my way.

A few months ago, I came across the book and noticed the inscription which I had long forgotten.

"Thomas, Always serve."

A best-selling author and the founder of the greatest fast-food restaurant have advice for all of us: "Always serve."

...but through love serve and seek the best for one another.
Galatians 5:13 AMP

The Generosity Factor
©2002 Ken Blanchard and S. Truett Cathy

DID YOU EVER PRAY FOR ME?

An often-forgotten element when praying for health and healing.

As a believer new to the Spirit-filled life, I was eager for instruction and guidance.

Like many life lessons, one element of my training came unconventionally.

I was working in a building owned by a doctor whose office was next door to our office.

He wasn't the *sport coat and necktie* type of doctor. One day, he said, "These Christian people come to my office asking me to help them feel better. Then they tell me, "I am praying, asking God to heal me." I ask them, "Do you ever pray for me?"

His statement hit me hard as I realized I had never prayed for any doctor.

Since then, I have prayed for the doctors, nurses, and attending staff at every hospital call and doctor's appointment. I ask God to bless them and help them by bringing things to their memory that are needed to aid in healing. My prayers also include asking God to bless their families, their practice, and their finances and give them peace and favor with their patients.

Through the years, I have expanded my prayers to include those who work on my car, prepare my taxes, and represent me in my profession.

God uses many avenues to bring health and healing to us. Sometimes, He uses doctors. Let us make a conscientious effort to pray for and bless those who help care for us.

The one who blesses others is abundantly blessed;
those who help others are helped.
Proverbs 11:25 MSG

THE SECRET OF GROWTH IS TO THINK SMALL

"Focus on people more than money. Without employees and customers, you're going nowhere. Make sure you never stop thinking about the customer's perspective." –David Green, *Hobby Lobby*

While managing radio and television stations, I quoted the phrase:

"We build our audience one (listener or viewer) at a time."

As a Television Station General Manager, I would make house calls helping our viewers with their television, antenna, or cable box. I carried tools and antennas in my car to help those who wanted to watch our programming.

During my corporate life, I told our staff: "Survey our customers--ask their opinion."

In the colleges and universities I taught and led, I repeated this phrase: "Without students, we do not have jobs!" (Imagine the impression when I told students this phrase! It is transformational.)

As we lead our churches and ministries, we build the Kingdom one person at a time.

One telephone call, one handwritten note, one post or tweet—our church is built one contact at a time. Want a larger church? Want a larger business? Think smaller—not larger.

1. Look for those who no one else is looking for.

2. Survey the people you serve. Ask what you do well and how you can do better. Ask for suggestions.

3. Empower the forgotten, the lonely, the disenfranchised. This silent army is waiting to serve and feel connected.

4. Celebrate the smallest victories.

5. Create an environment where (customer) service is king. Be the Chick-fil-A of your denomination, ministry, or business.

6. Help someone in secret. Buy a meal, mail a book to someone anonymously, bless someone without taking credit.

7. Give people a reason to return. Do whatever you do in such a way that people can't wait to return.

NOT INSIGNIFCANT

And these all, having obtained a good report through faith, received not the promise: God having provided some better thing for us, that they without us should not be made perfect.
Hebrews 11:39-40 KJV

Most Christians enjoy reading Hebrews 11, the Hall of Fame of Faith and Who's Who of the Patriarchs. How could you feel otherwise? It is a chapter filled with the story of how people in adverse conditions were miraculously healed, delivered, or accomplished something great for God. While it is true many of these lost their lives for their faith, their testimony has encouraged millions throughout the years.

I have often wondered when our time on earth has ended if those we leave behind will say we accomplished great things for God.

Notice the final two verses of Hebrews 11. No matter how great these people were, they had not received the better way of Jesus.

Should we think of ourselves as insignificant, the concluding verse of Hebrews 11 reminds us "they without us should not be made perfect."

In the Kingdom of God, we need the patriarchs *and* modern saints for God's plan to be complete.

Let's stand in faith!

THE SENIORS BUFFET

You should visit the Seniors Buffet at least once each month, if only to see how the golden and silent generations experience life.

On a recent visit I observed the following interactions:

Two US veterans ask each other about their military experiences, and where they were stationed. Both made it back safely.

Our server sits at the table of a veteran eating all by himself. She provides not only conversation, but technical support to help him program his iPhone.

Seniors eating alone are captivated by babies and toddlers. In fact, it works both ways.

My heart was full, and my eyes were misty.

Please do not forget these, the greatest of generations.

Wisdom may be found in the company of the aged.
Understanding comes with longevity.
Job 12:12 ISV

This photo was taken by a kind soul, an unknown fellow Christmas shopper at Bass Pro Shops.

OUR OWN PERSONAL TREE OF LIFE

The tongue that brings healing is a tree of life,
but a deceitful tongue crushes the spirit.
Proverbs 15:4 NIV

When we speak into someone's life, we bring healing to their situation. Our words convey hope and encouragement.

Think of your words as a form of currency. Use words to help put a smile on the faces of those around you.

Examples:

- "Being around you energizes me!"
- "I am glad you are here."
- "I am proud of you!"
- "I love how you ..."
- "I prayed for you today."
- "May God reward your efforts!"
- "You make the world a better place."

Let us bless others with our words, texts, telephone calls, and handwritten notes.

THE MERRY-GO-ROUND OF LIFE

We all face challenges. Our emotions and thoughts swing far left, then far right, then hopefully come to center point. During these challenges I am comforted by the fact that God does not change—regardless of our circumstances or feelings.

It seems that each of us have certain stressful times in our lives when the merry-go-round of life spins frenetically. We may be tempted to leave the ride because of its stress. However, that is the worst time to leave the ride!

My friend, whatever life's challenges are for you today--please know God has not changed.

He will strengthen and deliver you. He cares for you and wants the very best for every single day of your life!

For I am the Lord, I change not.
Malachi 3:6 KJV

WE ARE GOD'S ORCHESTRA

David summoned all the leaders of Israel, together with the priests and Levites. All the Levites who were thirty years old or older were counted, and the total came to 38,000. Then David said, "From all the Levites, 24,000 will supervise the work at the Temple of the LORD. Another 6,000 will serve as officials and judges. Another 4,000 will work as gatekeepers, and 4,000 will praise the LORD with the musical instruments I have made.

1 Chronicles 23:2-5 NLT

These verses give us an inside look into the administration of ministry by the Levites. 24,000 administered worship in the temple, 6,000 appointed as officials and judges, 4,000 security team and 4,000 were set aside for the orchestra.

On occasion my wife and I attend symphony concerts. I noticed how much the church is like the orchestra. We take our cues from the conductor as we all follow the same musical score. Some musicians are involved in every measure, others only for brief measures and some only a single note.

The conductor focuses his attention on the most critical components of the score—yet he is keenly aware of the others who play a supporting role or are resting for their moment—awaiting their turn. They are all members of the orchestra, they are all important and needed, they work together, and they yield their individual talents to the conductor who brings out their most excellent ability.

You might find it interesting to note as well that while the Levites spoken of in First Chronicles were from that specific tribe chosen as the only ones God would use as His priests, Peter later gave us an update. Believers in Jesus have now been added to that august group! "…You are royal priests, a holy nation, God's very own possession…" 1 Peter 2:9 NLT

My friend, no matter where you are in the concert God is orchestrating—you are necessary, important, and talented. You are highly favored.

WRITE THE VISION

...Write this. Write what you see. Write it out in big block letters so that it can be read on the run. This vision-message is a witness pointing to what's coming. It aches for the coming—it can hardly wait! And it doesn't lie. If it seems slow in coming, wait. It's on its way. It will come right on time.

Habakkuk 2:2-3 MSG

Photo by Kathy Harrison (circa 1989)

The author at his dining room table in Broken Arrow, Oklahoma writing *thank you* notes.

THE ROOM ERUPTED IN APPLAUSE

On this occasion, the applause was not the result of my speaking or performance.

As I entered a college cafeteria, I greeted an international student working at the cash register whose duties included placing silverware in small paper envelopes. But before I could catch my breath, a tray of silverware came crashing to the floor in a thunderous clang. (Presumably the young woman did not have a firm grasp on the silverware tray.)

I had a choice to make; either look at the woman in an accusatory glance or quickly find another option, then...I bowed three times to acknowledge the applause from the cafeteria crowd.

I decided to take the blame for the crashing silverware. The cashier was nonplussed.

To be honest, I got a kick out of the laughter and applause.

As I enjoyed my lunch and table conversations, I endured (and rather savored) ribbing by those present. A guest pastor leaned over to me and said I should be more careful.

I told him, between us, this is what happened. As I relayed the story, he smiled. Our discussion ended with "I would never want that woman to feel embarrassed."

Is it important who is to blame for silverware falling to the floor? If it is, God help us!

Isn't that what Jesus did? He who knew no sin became sin for us.

(2 Corinthians 5:12)

MEASURE TWICE, CUT ONCE

Lee was my intern when I served on staff at a megachurch. Since that time, he has become a trusted friend. He was a former military officer, and exudes the values of service and excellence.

Recently Lee moved to a new house in a new town and thus was church shopping. His first visit was to a church around the corner from where he lived. Tree branches from an adjacent property scratched cars in the parking lot. It was rumored the owner of the property was antisocial and did not want anyone to mess with the trees.

Later, Lee knocks on the owner's door (with pruning equipment in hand), introduces himself, and announces he was there to prune the trees interfering with the church, asking if he could trim anything else while he was there.

Turns out the owner was half-blind needing someone to help him—several problems solved with one act.

Sometimes things are not as we first imagine. How many times have we thought one thing, even repeated the same thing to another, only to discover we were in error.

My friend, Bud, was the first to tell me, "Measure twice; cut once." It's a basic carpentry and mechanical rule. It has saved me much trouble when I have heeded its meaning.

Let us prove things before we proclaim them as truth.

Prove all things; hold fast that which is good.
1 Thessalonians 5:21 KJV

THOSE WHO SPEAK THE LEAST OFTEN HAVE THE MOST TO SAY

While researching an organization for a consulting project, I conducted numerous one-on-one interviews asking for opinions and observations.

Research in general is as much a science as it is an art. I can speak academically about research as I have no less than 12 hours of research credits in my masters and doctoral programs. My masters thesis and doctoral dissertations were based on interviews and research.

My favorite research style? Interviews. My work in radio and television talk shows offered me opportunities to ask questions to the wealthy, influential, spiritual, and average citizens.

Here's something I gleaned from those interviews: those who speak the least often seem to have the most to say.

Want to improve yourself and your organization? Ask questions.

To be effective, one must have an element of trust, or the interviewee will not respond openly. If you announce "I am conducting research, and you are next to be questioned," your results will be flawed.

Research is best conducted in settings which your interviewee will find familiar and casual. Invite someone to walk with you, run a quick errand, pick up a snack at the drive through or perform a small task. "Can you help me carry this to the trash?" can become a casual interview.

In these casual settings, ask open-ended questions such as:

- "What can we do better in our church?"
- "If you were the president of (our organization), what would you do?"
- "Help me please; how can I be a better (pastor, supervisor)?"

Seek the opinions of office staff, custodians, those who seldom talk outside their ordinary circles. Ask the opinions of your "customers."

Through the years I leaned on the observations of a cafeteria worker and a hairdresser. They were listeners and knew what was happening in the organization and community. They freely gave me updates which I otherwise never would have known.

There are thousands of books and seminars to help us become better communicators. While such might be helpful, most of us could improve our knowledge by researching and listening.

We should also ask this question often: How can I become better?

WALTER

Perhaps it was the fajitas I had for dinner so late one night, but I had the most amazing dream I must share with you.

The setting was a casting call for a television program. What my purpose was, other than as an observer, is unclear.

A Cherokee woman enters the room with her young son, perhaps 12 years old, who was to audition. In my conversation with this boy, he was delightful and charming. A little shy, but otherwise, nothing negative stood out about this young aspiring actor.

The lead actor in the production, who governed the audition, was the epitome of arrogance. It seemed nothing was good enough for his standards. He took one look at the boy and promptly refused to audition him for the part. "He's not what we need. He does not look the part. He has no experience." With each statement the seasoned thespian's words cut like a knife. Everyone in the room felt the tension and naturally all eyes were on the young man whose only fault was not being the preferred choice for the audition.

At that point something came over me. I went to the young man putting my arm around his shoulders, and the two of us moved to place ourselves directly in front of the lead actor.

"As a seasoned actor, you have an obligation to provide your fellow actor with an opportunity to audition. As a seasoned actor it is your responsibility to provide feedback on the audition to this young man.

This boy has a face. This boy has a voice. Let us hear his voice. This boy has a name … his name is Walter!" With a boldness I have never seen before, I pled Walter's case. With each statement my voice grew louder, and my intense delivery was firm but not unkind.

I awoke and came to the computer to write what I had seen in the dream. I do not proclaim this was a dream from the Lord, again, perhaps the result of spicy Mexican food.

As I write these lines early this Saturday morning, I remember how many times we may be one of the characters in this dream. The part we play is often our choice. The loving mother provides transportation and gentle encouragement for her son's acting aspirations. We may be the featured actor whose mind is made up. It is our way or the highway. We can be the one who intercedes for others with a face but without a voice.

Walter, in the dream, was unfazed by the sharp criticism. It is possible Walter had heard similar phrases before. Without another intervening in the situation, Walter and his mother would return to their humble home, another opportunity denied.

Pleading the case for another is everyone's responsibility. I have told my nieces and nephews to look for the loner in school and church settings. Be a friend to the friendless.

God in his holy dwelling is a father of the fatherless and a champion of widows. God provides homes for those who are deserted. He leads out the prisoners to prosperity, but the rebellious live in a scorched land.

Psalm 68:5-6 CSB

Let us look for the Walters around us.

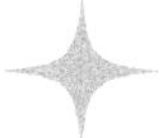

PULL THAT WEED

I passed by the field of a sluggard, by the vineyard of one who lacks sense. I saw that thorns had grown up all over it, the ground was covered with weeds, and its stone wall was broken down.

Proverbs 24:30-31 NET

The little things we ignore today will become the things we absolutely cannot ignore tomorrow.

May God help us to clean our closets (both the physical ones and the figurative ones). May we pull the weeds in our yards and … well … the other ones. May we mend our fences and speak to the stranger.

WE ASK IN FAITH

But you must learn to endure everything,
so you will be completely mature and not lack in anything.
If any of you need wisdom, you should ask God,
and it will be given to you. God is generous
and won't correct you for asking.
James 1:4-5 CEV

As people of faith, we realize we have the things we need when the time comes. If we lack anything, we ask God who gives to everyone and does not withhold.

WHEN DEATH COMES

I remember an occasion where two friends experienced the loss of a family member: one his wife and the other his mother.

Death for the Christian is a promotion to heaven.

Grief and loss are natural responses to the death of a friend, spouse, parent, or sibling. How can we help our friends and family during these times?

Prayer. Ask God to bring comfort and healing.

Communication. Let them know you care. Send a card with a handwritten message. Text often and ask about their wellbeing. Remind them of your love. Speak of the legacy and accomplishments of their loved one.

We would be wise to avoid the following actions:

Silence (We don't know what to say so we say nothing.)

Awkwardness ("I can't imagine what you are going through." "If you need anything, call me.")

Theological weirdness ("God must have needed an angel, so He took your relative.")

Be real. Be a friend. Be present (if you can). Communicate often.

Your friend may never remember what you say; they will always remember you were present at their time of need.

I want to enable you to appropriately respond at the time of death of a friend or relative. This resource is my recommendation to send with a card and your best wishes and prayers.

When You Lose Someone You Love by Richard Exley

A friend is a friend at all times…
Proverbs 17:17 NABRE

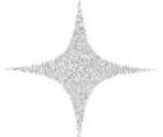

WEAK HANDS?

A veteran missionary to Northern China and I were talking recently when he suddenly stopped our conversation and said: "Thomas, many people give up too soon."

As soon as I heard that I knew it was the subject of this article. Perseverance is an old-fashioned word and seldom is used to describe modern society. "Persistence in doing something despite difficulty or delay in achieving success." (The Oxford Dictionary)

But you, take courage!
Do not let your hands be weak,
for your work shall be rewarded.
2 Chronicles 15:7 ESV

My friend, we may be tempted to give up; the rewards are ahead *if* we hold on to God and His plan for our lives.

Photo by Christina Bullard

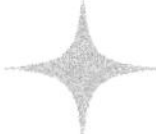

TURN THE LIGHTS ON!

Recently I purchased a Maglite™ Flashlight with an LED bulb. These are favored by law enforcement personnel because they can be used as a weapon and are practically indestructible. A feature of the LED bulb is that it is so bright it can be used during the day where indoor lighting may fail to adequately illuminate.

During one challenging week, various situations in my life were such that the gifts of Discerning of Spirits, the Word of Knowledge and the Word of Wisdom (1 Corinthians 12) were needed in abundance. People and situations are not always as they appear. On the surface,

I was troubled by several events.

Lamenting to my wife one evening (with details omitted) she reminded me of a prayer she has named: "God turn the light on:"

We know the entrance of God's word brings light.
Psalm 119:130

His word is a lamp to guide us.
Psalm 119:105

He is light in the darkness.
Matthew 5:14

God is my light and salvation.
Psalm 27:1

Evil vanishes in the presence of The Light. The Gifts of the Spirit are given to the believer to use—not just at church—but at home, in business, and in our private moments.

The next time you are perplexed or dismayed regarding what may or may not be true, ask God to turn the light on.

OUR WORDS ARE CURRENCY

When we exchange information or have a casual conversation, the words we speak are transactional; similar to paying the bill at a restaurant.

When we encourage or give someone a sincere compliment, it is the equivalent of giving someone a trip or an expensive gift.

Like apples of gold in settings
of silver is a word spoken in right circumstances.
Proverbs 25:11 NASB

HELPING OTHERS SUCCEED IS THE HIGHEST FORM OF LOVE

At one time or another, just about everyone has felt like the new kid on the first day at a new school. But we can choose to be the friend who comes to the rescue at a critical moment. We can be the difference between success and failure.

Let us help others succeed.

There is someone in your network who needs a good friend to help them succeed.

Use your talents, connections and resources to bring them to the next level.

… I was a stranger, and you invited me into your home….
And the King will say, 'I tell you the truth,
when you did it to one of the least of these my
brothers and sisters, you were doing it to me!'
Matthew 25:35-40 NLT

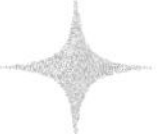

THE RAREST

The rarest stable metal is tantalum.

The rarest metal *on earth* is actually francium, but because this unstable element has a half-life of a mere 22 minutes, it has no practical use.

Among the rarest elements in society is thankfulness. It seems passé to thank someone or offer praise.

Because that, when they knew God, they glorified him not as God, neither were thankful; but became vain in their imaginations, and their foolish heart was darkened.
Romans 1:12 KJV

Let us do our part to make thankfulness and gratitude more common in society.

YOU ARE ANOINTED

At the moment of salvation, believers are indwelt by the Holy Spirit and joined to Christ, the Anointed One. (Acts 2:38) As a result, we partake of His anointing. (2 Corinthians 1:21-22)

But you have an anointing from the Holy One [you have been set apart, specially gifted and prepared by the Holy Spirit], and all of you know [the truth because He teaches us, illuminates our minds, and guards us from error].
1 John 2:20 AMP

So ...

God shows unfailing kindness to His anointed.
Psalm 18:50 NIV

God shows steadfast love to His anointed.
Psalm 18:50 ESV

God shows loving devotion to His anointed.
Psalm 18:50 BSB

God is doing kindness to His anointed.
Psalm 18:50 YLT

Be encouraged today, knowing God has rewards for His anointed.

WHEN ANSWERS AREN'T ENOUGH

My friend, this song tells a story, perhaps it's your story.

Details known only to God are the best approach when you have been betrayed, and your heart and spirit are wounded and broken.

Trust God again, one more time.

When Answers Aren't Enough

You have faced the mountains of desperation.
You have climbed,
You have fought,
You have won;
But this valley that lies coldly before you
Casts a shadow you cannot overcome.

And just when you thought you had it all together
You knew every verse to get you through;
But this time the sorrow broke more than just your heart
And reciting all those verses just won't do.

When answers aren't enough, there is Jesus.
He is more than just an answer to your prayer.

And your heart will find a safe and peaceful refuge;
When answers aren't enough, He is there.

Instead of asking why did it happen
Think of where it can lead you from here.
And as your pain is slowly easing, you can find a greater reason
To live your life triumphant through the tears.

When Answers Aren't Enough

AWESOME AND WONDROUS

By awesome and wondrous things You answer us in righteousness, O God of our salvation. You who are the trust and hope of all the ends of the earth and the farthest sea.

Psalm 65:5 AMP

In the coming days, expect your prayers to be answered in *awesome and wondrous* ways as you trust God.

ON ASSIGNMENT

We are walking miracles and testimonies of God's protection, deliverance, and blessings.

We are walking miracles? Yes!

Think of what had to occur for you to be reading this.

Our ancestors survived floods, famine, wars, poverty, plagues, recessions, depressions, political upheaval, so-called "natural" disasters, and a host of other occurrences which we will never know or understand.

Our DNA has survived centuries which helped bring us to today.

As surely as we are alive today, God has saved us for a specific assignment.

Whatever your assignment, praise God you are here to complete that assignment.

We must be mindful that we are divinely appointed and Spirit anointed to complete a specific assignment.

This reminds me of a sign I saw in the office of Pastor Vep Ellis, Jr.

"I was put on this earth to accomplish a certain number of things for God. Right now, I am so far behind, I will never die."

Seriously, we must be about the Father's business as Jesus told His earthly parents in Luke 2:49.

You are on assignment today!

God has made us what we are. He has created us in Christ to live lives filled with good works that he has prepared for us to do.
Ephesians 2:10 GWT

YOU DO NOT HAVE TO BE A PRESBYTER

One day during a ministers' meeting, I asked God if I could serve in a particular elected position. The voice of the Lord came strong yet gentle, "You do not have to be a presbyter to act like one."

Serve whether elected or not. There is always a place for servants in the Kingdom of God.

Sitting down (to teach), He called the twelve (disciples) and said to them, "If anyone wants to be first, he must be last of all (in importance) and a servant of all."
Mark 9:35 AMP

Will you be available and serve?

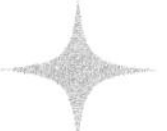

THE OPOSSUM

Heidi, Andy and their adult son, Stanley stood in line outside a buffet restaurant one Thanksgiving. In line behind this family was my pastor friend who began a conversation.

This family spoke of their lives to the pastor … living in a small building which they called home. No running water or modern conveniences.

"We are thankful for the opossum that came to live with us," Andy said, detailing how the marsupial took care of pest control which included various small reptiles that came inside the home.

The pastor prayed with them to find employment and that God would bless their family.

He gave them his telephone number and invited them to church.

The family was thankful for their new friend.

"I want you to have this," Andy said to the pastor and handed him a restaurant gift card.

The pastor was thankful but insisted the family might need the gift card more, yet Andy was insistent the pastor should accept the gift.

My pastor friend did not want to deny the family God's blessing. Giving is how we are blessed.

From their appearance, this family was practically the definition of poor, yet they freely gave of what material possessions they had—a restaurant gift card, most likely a gift from a kind soul.

Contrary to what one may assume, this family did not ask for a handout. It is doubtful any of us have experienced poverty on this level. I have never thanked God for an opossum that came to live in my house … well, or anything of the sort.

Friends, let us be truly thankful and generous. Let us be friends with those who others may ignore.

But the stranger who resides with you shall be
to you like someone native-born among you;
and you shall love him as yourself, for you were
strangers in the land of Egypt;
I am the LORD your God.
Leviticus 19:34 AMP

WAITING TO MEET NOAH

I am in line at Hobby Lobby, ready to check out. A long line of customers is assembled behind me. My turn to check out, and I am greeted by Noah, the Hobby Lobby employee.

ME: "Noah, you must be famous?!" (I have his full attention now.) "All these people behind me are waiting to meet you."

NOAH: "Something like that, sir." (As he chuckles.)

I understand it was Dale Carnegie who wrote: "There is no sweeter sound than one's name."

Friends, be generous with your blessings and use people's names when they serve you.

Photo by Kathy Harrison

Show respect for all people...
1 Peter 2:17 AMP

LIFE LESSON FROM A SALE BARN

As a young man, my grandfather was the wisest man I knew. Most summers my brother and I would spend a week or two on his farm in northwest Arkansas *helping*. One day, the three of us loaded goats into a truck to take them to the county sale barn. The goats were quite plentiful that year, and one can use only so many goats on a farm.

Sale barns were social events as well as a place to purchase livestock. As we entered the seating arena, I noticed an unusually dressed man who, in my pre-teenage mind, looked rather odd and acted rather odd as well. I made an unkind and unflattering comment about this man. My grandfather gave me *the look*. He firmly told me: "You know nothing about that man or his life. Be quiet." I realized I had invoked the correction of a man I adored. I was ashamed then, and now years later I am embarrassed that my remarks about another life-traveler were unkind.

What seemed to be an endless parade of farm animals passed the auctioneer. Finally, grandfather's goats were on display. Bids rang out like popcorn exploding. When the gavel sounded, the successful bidder stood—it was THAT man.

I learned a valuable lesson that day. Judge no man; as he could be the one buying your grandfather's goats. Fortunately, this man never heard my words, neither did he know the life lesson he taught me that day at the sale barn.

Do not judge by appearances,
but judge with right judgment.
John 7:24 ESV

Prejudice comes in all sizes, shapes, colors, and behaviors. While I have a finely defined belief system which governs my life, I have spent a lifetime trying to understand others who may be different.

Originally published in *Move Up! Don't Give Up!*

YOU NEED PEOPLE WHO BELIEVE IN YOU

"You need people who believe in you, see potential in you, and want to invest in your future.

To become the man God wants you to become, you need godly men to invest in you.

Sometimes this is a more formal long-term investment, and sometimes it's an informal, short-term investment. Most likely, you will need some of both."

© 2022 J. Josh Smith
The Titus Ten

LIFE-GIVING WATER FROM TWO WOUNDED ONES

Thomas Jonathan Pritchard was born near Atlanta, Georgia and was among the first in the area to enlist and defend the Confederacy at the age of 21. In doing so, he received a signing bonus of $50. While that does not sound like much, in today's wages such is the equivalent of nearly $19,000. A veritable fortune in 1862.

Thomas and his older brother, Marion, joined Company F (Browles) Regiment in 1862 and fought the following May at the battle of Bakers Creek (Champion Hill), Mississippi. Both Marion and Thomas were wounded. While Marion died, Thomas survived, yet in a manner which will undoubtedly surprise you.

Thomas was wounded when a small musket ball from a round of gunfire slammed into his face at the base of his nose then exited behind his ear, causing him to lose the vision in one eye. A Union soldier noticed Thomas fall and against all logic, crossed the line of fire working his way to retrieve Pritchard's wounded body.

This unknown Union soldier placed Thomas on a cart taking the canteen from a mortally wounded soldier to help Pritchard. Having stabilized him, the Union soldier made his way across the firing line and rejoined his company.

What would possess a man to have such compassion for someone he didn't know, an enemy soldier? It defies logic or explanation.

News of Private Pritchard's wounds reached his wife who travelled by train from Atlanta to Champion Hill and lovingly treated her husband's wounds with her silk handkerchief.

While it sounds strange to us today, following the Civil War there were annual "Blue-Gray" reunions when soldiers from both sides would gather and tell war stories. Corporal Thomas Pritchard was at one such reunion, reciting the story of his wounds at Bakers Creek. Granted, 162 years later this story is difficult to believe, yet Corporal Pritchard was regaling this story to all who would hear. He proclaimed that God had spared his life.

A passing Union soldier heard the story and stopped dead in his tracks ... asking Thomas where and when this event happened. Pritchard stated: May 16, 1863, at Bakers Creek (Champion Hill), Mississippi. The passing solider was none other than the man who crossed battle lines twice to save someone he did not know. Thomas was eternally thankful for a soldier he then learned was named Mr. Lewellen.

For obvious reasons, Pritchard and Lewellen became good friends. Yet the story was just beginning for it wasn't long before Mr. Lewellen married into the Pritchard family. The two who once fought on opposing sides of the war were then joined and began making new memories, raising their families together. Mr. Pritchard later became a pastor in the Mabelvale, Arkansas area.

I proudly proclaim that Thomas Jonathan Pritchard, the man in this story, was my great-great grandfather. Yet our family knew nothing of the story until after my father's passing. However, as a family we always looked to the Lewellen branch of the family as special people; yet we did not know why.

As striking as this story is, the reality of life is that it is a miracle any of us are here today.

We are walking miracles by the grace of God. If you woke up this morning and blood is circulating through your veins, God has a mission for you to accomplish.

Who was the mortally wounded soldier? The water in his canteen aided in saving the life of Private Thomas Pritchard and afterward, contributed to the establishment of families. That name is lost to history. Yet far more wondrous than that was the Man who freely and of his own accord also gave water. That One gave the water of life, that is, eternal life, and was also mortally wounded ... to save your life and mine.

...Whoever drinks of the water that I will give him shall never be thirsty; but the water that I will give him will become in him a fountain of water springing up to eternal life.
John 4:14 NASB

Thomas and Sarah Pritchard

THE LORD IS NEAR

May the Lord answer you in the day of trouble...
and defend you...
Send you help...
and strength...

May He remember all your offerings...

May He grant you according to your heart's desire
and fulfill all your purpose...

Now we know that the Lord saves His anointed;
He will answer you from His holy heaven

We will remember the name of the Lord our God...
We have risen, and stand upright...

May the king hear us when we call.

Amen

Based on Psalm 20 NKJV

YOUR MIRACLE IS WAITING!

"In the late fourteenth century... New College, at Oxford moved into their quadrangle, the first structure of its kind, intended to provide for the residents all that they needed. On the north side... the chapel and the great hall, beautiful buildings and, as you might imagine, the focus of life at the college.

In the middle of the nineteenth century, almost five hundred years later, the college hired architect Sir Gilbert Scott to restore the roof of the hall. The roof and the great oak beams that supported it had badly rotted. And so, representatives from the college with Sir Gilbert visited Great Hall Woods, in Berkshire, where they expected to find trees for replacement beams.

Sure enough, the replacements were standing there, planted a century before for just that purpose."

© 2009 Max DePree
Leadership Jazz

This reminds me of the book by Tommy Barnett: *There's a Miracle in Your House, God's Solution Starts with What You Have.* (1996)

What do you need from God?

The answer to your prayer may be near you, waiting to be discovered and deployed.

Then the LORD said to him,
"What is that in your hand?"
"A staff," he replied.
Exodus 4:2 NIV

Dear God, help me to discover your provision that everything I need I find in you. Amen

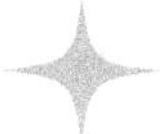

WHY THE ANSWER DID NOT COME

We have prayed earnestly, and our prayers were not answered. We quoted every Bible verse and stood in faith, but the healing did not come. Family and friends joined us and agreed in faith with us; however, the results did not change.

While in public, we quote the often-familiar lines: "God has a better plan for us ahead" or "We must trust God for the answer, not just our solution." In reality, we hurt. We may have been disappointed. No matter how we spiritualize it, the painful truth is that our prayers were not answered.

Please resist accepting personal responsibility for unanswered prayer. It is doubtful any of us have much control over that. It is also questionable there was sin or unbelief in our heart, or we would not have trusted God with our prayers and had faith in the first place.

Was God trying to punish us? I doubt that.

Is He going to help us—Most definitely!

Sometimes God does not make sense to us. I cannot explain how He creates a beautiful rainbow or why He would instruct Jesus to spit in a man's eye to bring healing.

I choose to believe God even when I cannot explain His actions.

God can certainly do anything except lie, and I am in complete agreement with whatever He wishes to happen or not happen.

If all of my prayers are answered, or none of my prayers are answered, God is still God.

The reality is: God answers more of our prayers than we give Him credit for.

We cannot always find a path from our prayers to the expected and manifested answer.

I am okay with that as well.

Like you, I have prayed for several things which have not been granted. Ah … but perhaps we should be thankful not all of our prayers were answered.

My friend, hold onto what you know is true: God loves you. Jesus died for you. We know prayer and faith in God work, and we will continue to pray!

Rejoice always, pray without ceasing,
give thanks in all circumstances;
for this is the will of God in Christ Jesus for you.
1 Thessalonians 5:16-18 NIV

Photo by Teddy Wyatt

Thomas, Kathy, and Jasmine

CAPITULUM FINALE*

Authors may obsess over the first and last pages of their book. The first page must capture the reader's attention; the last page resolves the author's quest and provides resolution and closure for the reader.

When faced with the challenge of the last story, I want the reader to hear my heart as I write these lines of *Oxygen For The Soul.*

When I was dating Kathy, we were both students at Arkansas State University in Jonesboro, Arkansas. I had recently begun my media career at KSOH Radio in North Little Rock, Arkansas as assistant manager, program director, early-morning and mid-day radio announcer (you get the idea).

Kathy was a member of Chi Alpha, the college campus ministry of the Assemblies of God.

The ASU chapter was sponsoring a Gospel concert as an outreach to the students, featuring the talented Andraé Crouch, who by this time had written and recorded numerous Christian songs and made appearances running the gamut between *The Johnny Carson Show* and Carnegie Hall.

Kathy asked me to emcee the concert due to my background in media and distinctive radio voice, as well as my recent position with a Christian radio station. That evening's concert launched a career of my working with Christian authors, ministers, pastors, musicians and business leaders.

Andraé Crouch wrote his first song at the age of 15, *The Blood Will Never Lose Its Power,* which now appears in numerous church hymnals and has been recorded by dozens of artists. For me, the most touching of Andraé's music has been *My Tribute* (subtitled *To God Be The Glory*).

My praise to God and my gift of thanksgiving for His blessings are found in the words of this song. Perhaps this is your prayer and praise to God as well as mine.

My Tribute

How can I say thanks
for the things You have done for me?
Things so undeserved,
yet You gave to prove Your love for me;
the voices of a million angels
could not express my gratitude.
All that I am and ever hope to be,
I owe it all to Thee.

To God be the glory,
to God be the glory,
to God be the glory
for the things He has done.

With His blood He has saved me,
with His power He has raised me;
to God be the glory
for the things He has done.

Just let me live my life,
let it be pleasing, Lord to Thee,
and if I gain any praise,
let it go to Calvary.

With His blood He has saved me,
with His power He has raised me;
to God be the glory
for the things He has done.

*The Final Chapter (Latin)
https://en.wikipedia.org/wiki/Andra%C3%A9_Crouch

HELP ME UP BEFORE YOU GO

One Saturday morning in July my wife and I worked in our flower beds, arising at 6:00 to work before the heat drove us indoors. And before the reader assumes anything, please understand that landscape and gardening work are at the top of my list of *least* favorite activities.

I was anxious to complete this task and get on with my usual Saturday activities (taking recycled materials to the recycling center, grading assignments, and working on my book projects) — basically anything to keep me anywhere except outdoors.

My wife was working on one area of the flower beds, and I heard her say: "Help me up before you go." She was seated on a plastic milk-carton type box and needed a little extra assistance.

The remainder of the morning I could not get that phrase out of my mind: "Help me up before you go."

I asked myself, have I helped my wife since we've been married? Have I improved her life? Have I helped her in society, financially, with her career and her musical endeavors? If I were to be taken to Heaven, could I say I have helped my wife?

Having cared for elderly relatives in my childhood home and in nursing homes, I am keenly aware of how life can twist and turn. As a pastor I have helped dozens of families through times of illness and the loss of their family members.

Dear Reader, have you prepared for your final moments on this earth? It is good to have plans for the distribution of your assets, and how you wish your final moments to be managed. How you choose to be remembered is largely in your hands. Live a good life and leave behind specific instructions, (along with finances, insurance, and legal documents) for those who will be responsible for managing your affairs once you leave this world.

It has always been my heart's desire to leave and go to Heaven. Wishing will not make that a reality.

The main message of this book is that God created you, He loves you and has provided a place for you to live with Him in Heaven.

There is only one way to Heaven, and that is through the Son of God whose name is Jesus. God created us and loves us so much He provided a way for us to be with Him in Heaven when we die.

For God so loved the world, that he gave his only Son,
that whoever believes in him should not perish but have eternal life.
For God did not send his Son into the world to condemn the world,
but in order that the world might be saved through him.
John 3:16-17 ESV

But God shows his love for us in that while
we were still sinners, Christ died for us.
Romans 5:8 ESV

If you declare with your mouth, "Jesus is Lord," and
believe in your heart that God raised him from the dead,
you will be saved. For it is with your heart that you believe
and are justified, and it is with your mouth that
you profess your faith and are saved.
Romans 10:9-10 NIV

If you would like to receive the free gift of salvation through Jesus, please pray this prayer with me. (Praying this prayer alone will not save you, but praying in faith that God will hear you will be the way to know you have eternal life in Jesus.)

> *Father God, in the mighty name of Jesus, I come to you today confessing I am a sinner. I have sinned in my heart and mind, and I know my only hope is in Jesus. I ask you, Jesus, to come into my heart, forgive me of my sins, and make me clean. I want to live in Heaven with you. I turn my back on my past and my sinful ways. I know if I call out to you, you will hear me. I am sorry for my life, but I wish to begin a new life in Jesus. God, please help me!*
>
> *With sincerity and honesty in my heart, I confess I am a child of God, and my sins have been forgiven.*
>
> *Amen*

Dear Reader, if you have prayed this prayer, God heard you and recorded your name in Heaven. Doesn't that sound amazing?

The next step is for you to tell someone of your decision; perhaps your spouse, friend, a pastor or me.

I encourage you to find a Bible-believing church to help you walk in the new path God has for you. If you need help finding a church, or would like to tell me about your decision, please send me an email. I would love to hear from you!

I want to help you up before I go.

Thomas Harrison, Ph.D.
thomas@mediaembassy.com

ENCOURAGEMENT AND INSPIRATION FROM CHRISTIAN LEADERS

A CHURCH BUILT BY CRAZY FAITH
Rodney Hutcheson

God placed a ministry calling on my life when I was a teen, but moving to a higher level that required "Crazy Faith" came after college graduation. I remember the moment sitting in a fireworks stand one summer day when God spoke to my heart. God had placed inside me a burning desire to win lost people to Jesus in the small town of Temple, Oklahoma.

At the age of 22, I entered a faith journey that few understood. I had no church planting training, no financial support, and no pastoral experience, but I had a word from God and some "Crazy Faith" to see the impossible! "Crazy Faith" is when you step out when others would say that is not a good idea. Peter demonstrated "Crazy Faith" when he stepped out of the boat while the storm was still raging. *Matthew 14:28-29 NLT, Then Peter called to him, "Lord, if it's really you, tell me to come to you, walking on the water." "Yes, come," Jesus said. So Peter went over the side of the boat and walked on the water toward Jesus.*

In the fall of 1990, The Assembly of God Outreach Center was started with a week-long schedule of services in the school cafeteria. Some thought I was testing the waters, but I was already committed to the word God spoke to me months earlier.

As a young man with childlike faith, I started looking for a church building that I knew God had already prepared. I located the old

Assembly of God building that had been closed for many years. This dilapidated church building was full of junk and trash. Some would have kept walking, but I knocked at the home next door to approach the owner. I obtained the building at a price that I could afford. Over the next few days, with hard work and lots of sprucing up, a house of worship was created for the people of Temple, Oklahoma.

I couldn't afford a mail out, but a young single man with "Crazy Faith" walked every street to invite others to experience God in a powerful way. I couldn't offer the programs or nice buildings that other churches were built on, but I knew God's Spirit would show up every week to transform lives of people who were serious about surrendering to God! I believed that His Spirit would draw people in, but it seemed unattainable to those who didn't understand the word God gave me. It was a church building where cables kept the walls from falling, water falls came when it rained, and gas fumes burned my eyes as I preached each winter because of the open-air heater. It shouldn't have worked, but people were being saved and lives were transformed each week.

In 1994, God honored the faith of a church planter by providing my partner in ministry. Sandra was not only my bride, but the worship leader we needed. Quickly, we began to pack out this building, and I knew God was directing us to build a new building. "Crazy Faith" was needed now more than ever!

We found property for sale behind the post office, and we set out to find the owner. I decided to test God by offering the owner $3,000, but she refused the offer because she said $300 was enough to purchase the property. While I'm not sure even my faith could have stretched quite that far, I learned that my God is never limited to my expectations. What a miracle!

Although we began with little funds, "Crazy Faith" remained alive and well in our hearts. We had building plans prepared by Sandra's cousin and were grateful to receive a $45,000 loan on the building from church headquarters.

Our plan was to use volunteer labor as we prepared to put our faith into action. RVers, (a volunteer building team of the Assemblies of God), and Department Of Correction inmates were ready to help us see our new church facility completed in 1996. We also had a church group in Missouri who planned to come and work for a week. After many attempts to arrive, the pastor finally called to let me know that the group would be unable to come. God knew we needed more finances than laborers, so the church sent us $10,000 to help us purchase additional supplies.

Some workers walked away from the building site after learning of our financial challenges, yet others like Bill Cole believed with me for the God-promised church building. Bill directed the construction of the building from the ground to completion. We kept adding more volunteer workers to our crew: a licensed electrician, a heat and air guy, a plumber from Texas, skilled workers, as well as general laborers. The day we put up our trusses may have been the greatest miracle because Pentecostals, Baptists, Methodists, Church of Christ, and a variety of believers from other denominations came together to complete the task.

We were getting closer to completing our building, but financial issues surfaced. "Crazy Faith" was needed more than ever! Our cabinet guy finally decided to donate all his work and supplies plus he decided to buy all the appliances and sinks! Fifty cent sheet rock miraculously became available! God used "Crazy Faith" to build a 5,000 square feet church building for $60,000!

"Crazy Faith" is believing God for miracles. It is when you become desperate, and you keep trusting God! In the tradition of Abraham, you "against hope believe in hope." You refuse to stagger at the promise of God through unbelief! You work to become strong in your faith … giving glory to God! (from Romans 4:18-20 KJV)

Oh yes, others may say you are crazy, but keep your focus on Jesus and watch as God uses your "Crazy Faith!"

Rodney Hutcheson has pastored four churches over the past 35 years. Pastor Rodney currently is leading his second church plant, Ignite Church, in Norman, Oklahoma. Rodney has a Master's Degree from Southern Nazarene University in Educational Leadership and serves currently as an administrator at a Christian school.

ignitenorman.com
rhutcheson@rocketmail.com

CAN SOMEONE WITH A HISTORY OF SPEECH IMPEDIMENTS REALLY HAVE A FUTURE IN MINISTRY?

Michael R. Scott

This is what I asked as a fifteen-year-old who just felt the call into ministry at a camp in a small Missouri town. I can take you to the exact spot on the left side of the former roller-skating rink-turned-campground tabernacle where I questioned God's choice of a future minister. I loved God as a teenager – I really did – and wanted to live my life for Him. But I also knew my weaknesses. So, in case God forgot, I was ready to remind Him of my three years of fairly intense speech therapy in elementary school to correct my mispronunciation of R's, L's, and S's. While those problems were mostly resolved by my teenage years, some words still came out wrong and, in my embarrassment, my face would turn redder than my hair. "God, I'll serve you. But there HAS to be someone else who is more qualified."

In Judges 6, God chose a man named Gideon to lead a small army against the Midianites, whose numbers the Bible compares to the grains of sand —far too numerous to count. Gideon, too, was quick to list his reasons why God should not use him: he was the smallest member of the weakest clan in the area, his father worshipped false gods, and anyone who was anyone was already out fighting while Gideon was left at home. God knew all the reasons why He should not use Gideon, and yet He still chose Him.

Why?

Why would God want to use a weak civilian to lead a small army against a military juggernaut? Why would God want to use a teenager with a history of speech problems to preach His Word? Why would God want to use you with your weaknesses, your past, and your background? Because when we depend on Him and find success, He is the only One who will receive the credit and the glory. Paul writes, "God chose the foolish things of the world to shame the wise; God chose the weak things of the world to shame the strong… so that no one may boast before him." (1 Corinthians 1:27,29 NIV). Our "victory" can only be attributed to an almighty God, who uses the weaknesses of the "unqualified" to accomplish the miraculous.

God used my insecurity about public speaking and turned it into a core aspect of my ministry. Through my "yes" as a fifteen-year-old in that camp tabernacle, God opened doors that I never would have imagined. I would go on to speak to tens of thousands of teenagers over the years as a youth pastor, camp speaker, youth ministry professor, and college vice-president in addition to serving as a public address announcer for high school and college athletic programs. The young teenager plagued with worry about misspeaking in front of a crowd would have never imagined the result of a simple "yes" to God and willingness to be used despite weaknesses. And the neat thing is that every time I speak to the crowd, it is a reminder that my God chose me to represent Him despite my weaknesses, and He miraculously empowers me to do what I cannot do on my own.

What is your weakness? What do you think disqualifies you from being used by God? What if, instead of letting your insecurities keep you from moving forward and moving up, you put them in the hands of our miraculous God, who knows exactly why He should not use you yet still chooses you? Trust Him with your weaknesses and make sure to give Him the glory when the victory happens!

Dr. Michael Scott recently returned to the world of full-time youth ministry after previously serving as a youth pastor, executive pastor, college vice-president, youth ministry professor, and Bible teacher. He is youth pastor at Central Assembly, Springfield, Missouri. He has a Doctor of Ministry degree in Next-Generation Ministry and enjoys life with his wife, Rebecca, and two children.

MichaelR.Scott@yahoo.com

FROM HEARTBREAK TO HOPE: A JOURNEY THROUGH INFERTILITY

Greg Wheat

For many, the journey of infertility is a hidden struggle, a battle fought silently in the shadows of despair. My wife, Janell, and I embarked on a decade-long quest to start a family, filled with heartache and unwavering hope. As we faced mounting medical bills and the agony of countless doctor visits, a recurring theme emerged—adoption. While I didn't totally oppose the idea, in those moments, it felt like a detour from what I believed was God's intended path for us.

One fateful day during a time of prayer, I sensed God whispering to me, assuring me that our prayers to have children of our own were being heard and that an answer was on the horizon. When I shared this message with Janell, her tears flowed—a blend of hope and relief enveloping her heart. Together, we began seeing specialists, embarking on fertility treatments. Each month, Janell's excitement would bloom, only to be met with crushing disappointment when her hopes were dashed. I held her tightly during those moments, her cries echoing my own heartache. "I thought you said God was going to bless us," she would plead. I clung to my faith, repeating our mantra: "I don't know when, but I know God will."

As the years passed, the pain deepened. Watching others who had children effortlessly felt like salt in an open wound. Janell struggled with the apparent injustice of it all, wondering if God loved them more than us. In those moments, I gently reminded her that God's love is unconditional and to hold on to the promise I believed He had spoken into my heart years prior.

After a ten-year journey, God answered our prayers and blessed us with our beautiful daughter, Kylie. But the desire to expand our family continued to grow, and we prayed fervently for another child—a son to continue our family's legacy. One day, while praying, I heard God once again reassuring me: "Don't mistake what seems overdue as being overlooked." I believed this promise, but as time wore on, doubt began to creep in. "Not now doesn't mean not ever" I would reassure Janell, as we held on to faith.

As the years passed, we did our best to forge ahead. Janell finally became pregnant with twins, and joy surged through our hearts. But then came the heart-wrenching news: one of the embryos had not survived. Our joy faded into sorrow, but we remained steadfast in prayer for the child still growing.

The journey took another alarming turn when Janell developed a severe infection, requiring hospitalization and the delivery of our baby—premature by several months. Standing by her side, I felt helpless while our baby boy was fighting for his life in the newborn ICU. Pressing my palms against the glass, I saw feeding tubes, oxygen tubes, and heart/lung monitors all connected to my little boy. With tears flowing down my face, I whispered to him, "You're strong, you can do this. Fight!" After a long battle, the day finally came when we could bring Kyston home. Our hearts swelled with gratitude as we held him tightly, aware of how fragile life can be.

I often reflect on our journey—the silent cries we had poured into the dark, the relentless faith that had spurred us on, and the whispered promises from God that marked our path. Through this entire experience, I've learned some invaluable truths about perseverance.

Life's challenges can sometimes feel overwhelming—rough, rocky, and towering like the tallest mountain. These struggles will test you—your strength, your faith, and your resolve. In my view, there are three essential things to have in life: God, grit, and good people.

Matthew 19:26 tells us that with God, all things are possible. Believe that you can overcome any struggle you face. With grit, keep moving forward, even if you have to crawl. Never give up!

It's also vital to surround yourself with people who will stand by your side through it all, offering encouragement and support. Don't try to face your challenges alone. Reach out to those who genuinely have your best interest at heart—those who will lift you up, someone you can lean on when needed, and who will help you across the finish line if they have to.

Greg Wheat holds a Bachelor of Arts degree in Church and Business and recently retired after more than 30 years of full-time ministry. Now an entrepreneur, he owns Thrive Early Learning Center, Fireworks Outlet OKC, and The Sweatshop Gym and Fitness.

Greg is also a speaker and the author of the new book *From Here to There: Getting from Where You Are To Where You're Meant To Be*.

A longtime community leader, Greg received the Purcell (Oklahoma) Citizen of the Year Award and continues to serve. He has served as a Chamber member for more than 8 years—including roles as board member and president.

He was also the president of Leadership Mid-America and currently serves on the Purcell City Council and the Purcell Tourism Board.

GregWheat.com

THE SOUL: PLEASE HANDLE WITH CARE

Nick Rogers

It began with a short sentence on my phone. I was invited to a free "Pastor's Only" retreat.

Wow!

It was a location with ocean breezes and sunshine. With glorious ethnic food and passport-necessary views. The accommodations were astonishing. The lottery ticket of this rural pastor had finally been drawn. How could this be happening? It was – unbelievable!

The trip was designed for those in ministry who were hardened by the gut-wrenching pressures of ministry and needed a chance to breathe—an opportunity to rest.

As I disembarked the plane with my carry-on and a slip of paper declaring my possessions, I failed to write down the following: sadness of the soul. You see, I had been running hard, pausing little, and was now reaping the consequences.

Once we settled in, we were then asked, "How are you? No, really, how are you?"

And then the group discussion started. It was deep and heart-wrenching. Evidently, the expense of saving souls is high.

And I found out at that moment in the discussion that my soul had much to say. My pastor friends and the Holy Spirit listened, then prayed, then spoke. I had not taken care of my own soul properly. Truthfully, it was damaged and needed to be lovingly mended.

Jesus states in Matthew 16:26b "…what will a man give in exchange for his soul?"

Poignant question from the Savior of the world directed to anyone willing to heed and reflect.

Indeed, what is a soul worth?

Why must the soul be handled so carefully?

I discovered I had cheapened the value of my soul. I hawked my soul to several ruthless benefactors: my expectations, my pride, my arrogance. I asked my soul to carry the burdens of others. Heal their wounds. Bind up their broken hearts. I fed my soul perfectionism, sleepless nights, and shots of dopamine. I brokered my soul to have a successful ministry.

I routinely told God I would help Him. My soul felt the blows of my independence.

I subjected my soul to striving and grinding. I would lower my head and put in another two hours, a phone call, and maybe an extra hospital visit to someone's relative I did not even know. Throw in a city council meeting, a snappy discussion with my wife, football practice with my son, and another dance fee for my daughter for good measure.

It was sheer folly and foolishness. I lived in deception. All the while, my battered *soul hurt.*

Can you relate?

I disregarded Jesus' question (from Matthew quoted above). But my soul – my soul loved and cherished by the Lord – felt the impact of days and months and years of toil. There was less time abiding (John 15). For when you abide, you are filled with heavenly resources.

There were fewer moments of green pastures and still waters (Psalm 23) and more moments of desert distress and rising tides.

I prayed to once again have "rivers of living water" (John 7:38) flowing freely, passionately out of my soul.

The next day was a beach day. It was an undeveloped beach far from the mainstay trappings of an average tourist on foreign soil. It was there that I discovered a hut full of surfboards and even a few instructors.

Surfing had always fascinated me. The sun, the sand, the iconic view of a guy standing up on a board in the middle of an infinitely-going ocean. And here in this moment was a bucket list opportunity for a guy who never ever expected this opportunity to happen.

Excited and still somewhat stunned, I rented a board for the day and a local instructor for one hour. I received a crash course in types of waves, when to commit to a wave, when to stand, and how to stand. It was exhilarating!

Surf movies and YouTube videos cannot capture the challenge of such an undertaking. It was so hard. The cardio was insane. The necessary coordination and the unique muscle groups essential to get on a floating device that sits upon moving water rising above more water. And then there is the repeated falling off the board. It never stops. And yet it was lighthearted fun necessary for a pastor's soul to begin healing.

That day. That trip, along with many small moments by myself and with my pastor friends, changed everything.

I began yielding my soul and its injuries to the Lord—one after another after another. For my anxious, anguished soul was known by God (Psalm 31:7). Truly, He does *restore my soul* (Psalm 23:3).

The question Jesus poses is often overlooked and dismissed, even though it's about victory and celebration and lasting joy. His joy!

It's a question that distinguishes the seasoned veterans of ministry from the starry-eyed newcomers of the recently called.

Proverbs 10:3a says, "The Lord will not allow the righteous soul to famish..." NKJ

I am slowly learning to protect my soul. To abide. To receive heavenly nourishment.

That four-day trip ended years ago. But the Lord and I still have a way to go.

Ah, but how is my soul, you ask? Yes, it is better as I continue to learn how to handle it with care.

And my surfing? I'm officially retired…at least until I happen to stumble upon another hut.

Since January 2018, Nick Rogers has held the position of District Youth and Kid Ministry Director for the West Texas District of the Assemblies of God. He also serves as the Executive Director of Roaring Springs Camp and Retreat Center.

Over the years, Nick and his family have contributed to various ministry roles, including volunteering, bi-vocational service, and full-time ministry positions. Their experience spans from new church start-ups to more established, legacy congregations, and most recently, nine years of senior pastoring in rural West Texas.

Nick holds a Bachelor's Degree in Church Ministries and a Masters of Science in Theological Studies from Nelson University.

He lives in Lubbock, Texas, with his lovely wife, Alicia and their children: Nash and Anna.

rogersnickw@gmail.com

NOTHING WILL BE IMPOSSIBLE

Eric B. Smith

Has God called you to do something big? Do you carry a heavenly directive that you won't be able to accomplish without His help? If so, it is helpful to remember that if God is for you and with you, nothing can stand in your way. While the Bible tells us that God empowers those He calls (Hebrews 13:20-21), it is easy to forget this vital truth, amid the battle. Understanding this is crucial because knowing He empowers the called should boost our faith, our willingness to take risks, and our fearless pursuit of the Kingdom of God. Truly, if God is for us, who can be against us? (Romans 8:31)

In 1914, A.B. Cox answered the divine call to preach the gospel and began spreading revival from Maryland to Oklahoma. He became a powerful minister, spanning decades of preaching and church planting. Cox, known for his fiery, unscripted preaching style, always concluded his messages with a call for sinners to repent and for believers to come and "tarry" for the Baptism in the Holy Spirit. To be Pentecostal in America in the early 1900's required dedication, as it was common for people protesting the church's existence to throw rotten eggs and tomatoes at preachers and parishioners alike as they left their churches after services concluded. Despite the religious prejudices of his day, preachers like A.B. Cox continued to boldly proclaim the gospel.

As an evangelist, Cox's meetings were often marked by people encountering God, with intense times of crying out that might last hours. In one revival meeting at a Maryland church, nightly crowds grew to around 500 in a small building. Neighbors complained and called the police about the noise from people praying and experiencing the power of the Holy Spirit.

When the police arrived, they arrested Cox. During his arrest, the son of the police chief, also a local bar owner, assaulted Cox, punching him in the head several times. This was likely due to preaching that contributed to the bar's shrinking customer base. However, Cox was released from jail a few hours later, and undeterred, returned to the service to find a large group of people who had remained and continued to pray. It was later reported that at least 18 people, including many church leaders, were baptized in the Holy Spirit that very night, despite police interruptions.

In 1918, Cox received a clear call from God and moved to Dayton, Ohio, a city in southwest Ohio. He later described this dramatic calling by saying God spoke plainly to him: "Dayton! Dayton!" He felt called to start a new church; however, God would use him for something much bigger. Cox and his wife, Dora, moved immediately to Dayton with no support system and no promise of income. When they arrived, he followed the plan God had given him. For the next three years, A.B. Cox worked as an electrician by day to pay the bills and preached seven nights a week. According to a tract Cox wrote at that time, his weekly schedule also included daily prayer meetings led by him or Dora. By today's standards, this schedule of ministry would be difficult to imagine, but for A.B. Cox, he was doing everything he could to fulfill his calling from God. During this time, the church experienced rapid growth, with many people being saved and baptized in the Holy Spirit.

At the height of revival, A.B. Cox invited a well-known evangelist to lead upcoming revival services. In May 1920, Aimee Semple McPherson visited Dayton, and God's power moved mightily, with many receiving healing and salvation. The revival's success was evident not only in the large crowds attracted by McPherson but also in the years of foundational prayer and subsequent follow-up discipleship led by Cox.

Despite opposition, a great awakening was taking place in the city; residents were discovering a deep hunger for God and marveling at the incredible things God was doing.

By the time Cox's ministry in the city concluded with his retirement in 1945, he had established 17 churches, a Bible college, and seen 73 people respond to the call to full-time ministry. More than a century after A.B. and Dora Cox moved to Dayton, he remains recognized as the father of the Pentecostal movement in Dayton, Ohio.

If you have a calling from God, what price are you willing to pay to see His will done in your community? Even if challenges seem insurmountable, you can move forward confidently, knowing that God is with you and will provide the strength you need. Our divine calling always authorizes us to work hard, dream big, and face any challenge. "For nothing will be impossible with God." Luke 1:37 NET.

Video Documentary of the 2014 Dayton meetings
https://youtu.be/R2fG_ch93-o?si=bg3usBN1-dBojssc

Eric Smith is a church planter, revivalist, pastor, and author. He is a husband, father, and grandfather, and holds a Master's Degree in Biblical Studies.

DestinyDayton.com
PastorEricSmith@proton.me

[1] Daphne Brann, "Those Early Pentecostal Days" (Unpublished Manuscript), 1994, 4.
[2] Watson Argue, "The Get Acquainted Page," *The Latter Rain Evangel*, March 1936, 13.

WHEN THE WORD IS OUR GUIDE

Lee Guidry

Walking along a mountain brook, my life was at peace. The temperature was perfect, the air fresh, and the sounds of chirping birds made the experience more surreal. As I walked along the brook, a bear charged out of the woods towards me. I stared in shock as he gained speed, drawing closer and closer. I could not move. Fear paralyzed me. At that moment, I knew I must make peace and take the inevitable. My life was ending here. I closed my eyes and waited for the oncoming attack. While waiting for the bear to attack me, I suddenly heard something. I opened my eyes and saw two dogs running towards me. Faster and faster they ran until they caught the bear and fought him off. I woke up.

Jumping out of bed in a cold sweat, I started pacing up and down the house. The dream was so real. Why was I there? Why would my brain give me this horrible dream? This would be the first of many times I would ask this question. Less than 24 hours prior, I had experienced one of the greatest fears a teacher can face: a school shooting. My mind was beginning to unpack the trauma I knew I would have to tackle.

On January 22, 2018, at approximately 7:58 am, I was making copies in the teacher's lounge, getting ready for the day. Suddenly, I heard what sounded like a banging noise and then students screaming. I looked out into the breezeway and saw a student standing over another student, waving a gun while screaming profanities. Without thinking,

I ran towards the gunman as students were running away. This was not some heroic move to save the day. I just felt this was what I had to do.

Once I reached the breezeway, I found myself face-to-face with the student/gunman. I had nothing with which to defend myself. At that moment, I remembered Proverbs 15:1 ESV, "A soft voice turns away wrath." I took a deep breath and asked, "Please back away; we will figure all of this out, but I need you to back away." I repeated this in a calm, soft voice three times before the gunman acknowledged me. After the third time of pleading my request, he turned and ran away.

When the gunman fled, I immediately went to the victim. She had been shot six times. As I was kneeling by her applying first aid, she cried, "Mr. Guidry, please don't let me die." I am not a medical doctor and did not know the damage the six bullets had caused. I did not know what to say. At that moment, Proverbs 15 came to my mind again. I remembered the beginning of verse 4, which states, "A gentle tongue is the tree of life," and I spoke to her in a calm voice saying, "You are not dying today." I kept repeating that to her until the first responders arrived. It seemed like an eternity, but something in me knew I was telling the truth. She would not die that day. What I said was not a lie; God gave me the words that would ring true that day.

In the following weeks, there was much emotional trauma to handle. The tragedy happened in the cafeteria right before the eyes of most of the students. Those young people needed someone to be strong for them. They often came into my classroom crying, needing someone to comfort them. Proverbs 15 continually went through my mind as students showed up, seeking comfort. It was all I could do to provide the help they needed.

May of 2023 was a milestone in this journey. The last students who had been on campus at the time of that horrific act graduated. They made it. During those years, I knew I was called to be an advocate for student safety and would need the academic credentials to lend credence to that calling. I enrolled in a doctoral program and received a scholarship that covered most of the cost. In 2021, I earned a Doctorate of Education in Curriculum and Instruction. I knew my time in the high school classroom was coming to a close and it was time for a new chapter in my life. In 2024, I accepted a professorship at Nelson University. I now have the opportunity to share my story while preparing the next generation of teachers.

Years have passed but the memory is fresh. For so long I had to be strong for others, and now it is time to be strong for myself. I wish I could say everything was fine and I am over it all, yet I'm not sure one ever totally gets over an event like this. You can, however, learn to cope with it. Psalm 91:4 ESV tells us that we will take refuge under His wings. I still have the nightmares, and the bear still comes for me, but the two faithful canines are always there to protect me. I believe they are put there by God to show that this evil will not consume me. It is how He brings me through the Valley of the Shadow of Death.

My story is not a story of tragedy, but one of healing. It is my prayer that my story is an encouragement to those going through emotional trauma. God is our emotional protector. Lean on Him and take refuge under His wings. Let your healing be an encouragement for others.

Lee Guidry, Ed.D., is an Associate Professor at Nelson University. He resides in Texas with his wife, Angie and his two children, Maddie and Nate.

DrLGuidry@Gmail.Com

FINDING YOUR RHYTHM AGAIN THROUGH ROUTINES

Jerry Edmon

Ever notice how most men start shaving in the exact same spot every morning? I do. And I'm willing to bet (if you're a man) you do too. We don't talk about it — there's no support group for habitual shavers — but it's one of those tiny, unconscious rituals that quietly hold our days together.

We are creatures of rhythm. Whether we admit it or not, our lives beat to a drumline of invisible habits. Brushing your teeth. Brewing the coffee. Driving the same route. Folding socks like your momma taught you. These things are small, but they're sacred. They tether us to structure, to sanity, and sometimes — to hope.

I remember falling out of my workout routine once. I told myself it was just a short break. (You know where this is going.) A week turned into a month, and before I knew it, the rhythm was gone. The gears were not jammed — they just weren't turning. My energy slipped. My focus thinned. I had tools, but no tempo.

Turns out, routines are more than productivity hacks. They're your internal metronome. They don't make the music, but they keep you on tempo so when the melody comes, you're ready to play.

Just like the surfer out on his board. From the shore, he looks like he's doing nothing. But he's not asleep — he's tuned in. He's reading the water, feeling the rise, anticipating the moment. Because when that wave finally swells, you don't get time to warm up. You just move. And the ones who move best? They stayed in rhythm.

Even the greats knew this. Ludwig van Beethoven, the genius with wild hair and bigger emotions, was famously precise about his habits. Every morning, he counted exactly 60 coffee beans for his cup. Then he sat at his desk and composed for hours. Storm outside? Meltdown inside? It didn't matter. He had a rhythm. And rhythm made room for brilliance. That may have seemed a bit neurotic, but it was what did the job for him.

I love how Winston Churchill kept his rhythm in the middle of WWII — literal bombs falling on London — still took his bath, read his newspapers, and maintained other daily rituals. Why? Because when the world gets loud, routine helps you hear your own thoughts.

Even the humble farmer, centuries before apps or alarms, knew that rhythm ruled the earth. He worked by seasons — planting, pruning, harvesting, rest. He didn't panic when winter came. He didn't get lazy in spring. He just kept rhythm with the soil.

You don't have to be brilliant, famous, or rural to get this. You just have to pay attention to the beat of your own life.

Routine reveals what's out of place. And when you've got nothing else to hold onto, routine holds you.

I've had quiet seasons. You probably have too. Times when it feels like nothing's moving forward. You start wondering if you missed your exit. You question your calling, your job, your location. "Maybe I'm done here?" "Maybe I need to find something else?" That's usually when you need to sit still the most.

Routine doesn't mean you're stuck. It means you're positioned. Set a wake-up time. Make your bed. Read one verse. Walk the same old sidewalk for a while and see what shows up. These aren't chores. They're lifelines. They don't fix everything, but they fix your focus — and that alone can save a season.

If you've lost your rhythm — and we all do, from time to time — don't try to fix everything at once. Just find one thing that used to bring you a sense of order or calm and quietly pick it up again. Maybe your routine is rising with the sun, walking the same path you once did, or lighting a candle before prayer. Don't wait to feel inspired. Let the act itself do the heavy lifting. Trust that repetition, that routine is not just memory's friend — it's the soil where purpose grows back. You won't feel the shift overnight but keep showing up. Keep the rhythm even when it doesn't sing. One day, without realizing it, you'll hear the music again. And it'll be yours.

And let me leave you with this... Even jazz, the most improvisational music on earth — wild, unpredictable, soulful — only works because of rhythm. Without rhythm, it's not genius. It's just noise.

So maybe it's time to stop waiting for your "next big moment" and just start moving to the beat again.

Your rhythm is still in there. Let's find it.

"...But then I will come and do for you all the good things I have promised, and I will bring you home again." Jeremiah 29:10 NLT

Since 1972, Jerry Edmon has dedicated his life to helping people confront the pressures of everyday life and overcome the hurdles that hold them back. Through clear insight, practical direction, and a prophetic anointing that has marked his ministry from its beginning, countless lives have been changed and redirected toward purpose.

Jerry provides pastoral oversight to Family Worship Center in Elgin, Texas, as well as to a network of relational churches. He also serves on the Board of Directors for the Independent Assemblies Fellowship of Churches and the Deliverance Temple International Fellowship of Ministers, and as an Advisory Board member for Clarion World Mission Organization.

Recognized as both an ambassador and strategist, Jerry's voice continues to inspire growth, clarity, and transformation in relation to life, leadership, and the Kingdom of God.

jerryedmon.com

"I'M 'SPOSE TO BE HEALED TONIGHT!"

Roberta Roberts Potts

… Your faith has saved you …
Luke 7:50 NIV

After he had prayed for so many people, my dad would be gut-wrenchingly tired. I don't know just how long some of those healing lines lasted. I don't know how many hurting, suffering people lined up in front of him, hoping so much for a miracle. But what I do know is that there came a time when Oral Roberts would be bone tired and there was just nothing else left for him to give.

Picture him standing there all that time. An hour? Two hours? Reaching out his right arm to pray, believing in faith with all his might for every single person who came before him. Sometimes children, sometimes adults. Sometimes people who could walk, sometimes individuals on crutches or maybe in wheelchairs. One particular evening after he'd prayed for sick folks for many long hours, there were many more people lined up — wanting so much to be prayed for — but he had no choice. There was nothing for it but to close the meeting for the night. The healing evangelist had proven once again that he was all too human and he had reached the end of what his little daughter saw, or rather imagined, as super human strength.

But on the way out to the car waiting to take him to his motel room, Dad met a little boy … an incredibly persistent little boy … perhaps

7 or 8 years old. From what Dad could later discover, the boy's mother had brought him to the crusade that night and they had been waiting in the healing line, but when Dad had been forced to stop, they had been left standing.

Undaunted, the little boy was far too determined to give up. When he saw that the evangelist was no longer praying for the sick, he disappeared, undoubtedly causing no small concern to his poor mother!

All Dad knew was that the little boy appeared before him saying: "Mister, I'm 'spose to be healed tonight!" Of course Dad began explaining, probably very kindly the first time, "Son, I preached a sermon, I had an altar call for the salvation of lost souls, I've been praying for the sick all evening, and the truth is, I'm just too tired to do anymore. I'm really sorry, but you and your mother will just have to come back tomorrow night."

But the little boy refused to leave. "Sir, I don't know anything about all that. All I know is that I'm 'spose to be healed tonight!" Now since he was my daddy —- especially now that he's in Heaven! — I can tell you that Oral Roberts had a little bit of a temper, especially when he was tired. And I wouldn't have had the nerve to cross him in that moment. No, not me! Knowing him as I did, I suspect Dad's reply was a little less than kind. But nothing he could say or do would change the mind of that little boy. He simply repeated: "I'm 'spose to be healed tonight!"

Finally in desperation, Oral Roberts placed his hands on the boy in a healing prayer, perhaps not including all that much faith. But ... yes, the little boy was correct. He was supposed to be healed that night and he WAS healed that night. It obviously had little to do with an exhausted evangelist. And the power that brought the healing did not reside in the boy either. The power came when a desperate faith met the same Jesus who healed the paralytic let down from a roof. (Matthew 9:2-8) Yes, he was 'spose to be healed. And it's that kind of faith, my dear sister, my dear brother that will heal you! Believe in faith today ... for that same Jesus who healed the little boy has not changed nor will He ever change!

Believe. Believe in His ever present healing power. It's for you. It's for you, today! I say to you right now in the name of Jesus, you're 'spose to be healed!

"When the crowd saw this, they were filled with awe; and they praised God, who had given such authority to men." Matthew 9:8 NIV

To learn more about the man and ministry of Oral Roberts, the reader may wish to discover the following resources:

Potts, R.R. (2011). *My Dad, Oral Roberts.* Icon

This remains the only biography of Oral Roberts written by a family member. The book features behind-the-scenes accounts of the man and ministry of Oral Roberts, including insights into songs used during tent meetings conducted by the Roberts crusades. You may order your copy through the website: https://www.robertapotts.com/my-book/

You may research the ministry of Oral Roberts by accessing printed material, photos, audio and video recordings through:

Flower Pentecostal Heritage Center https://ifphc.org/
Holy Spirit Research Center at Oral Roberts University
https://oru.edu/c4ser/holy-spirit-resource-center.php

For 25 years, Roberta practiced as an attorney in the State of Oklahoma representing individuals who were injured in motor vehicle accidents. As the younger daughter of Oral Roberts, Roberta grew up watching her father preaching and praying for the sick in vast healing crusades. Assisting hurting people not only seemed a natural extension of her father's healing ministry, but it also gave her an opening to pray for the sick as well.

Since that time she has written a book about her father (*My Dad, Oral Roberts*), assisted others with their writing projects and composed a number of devotional and teaching articles as well. For several years she has also assisted her pastor with sermon illustrations. Her newest project is Roberta's Research, reaching out to assist other pastors and authors as well.

She enjoys writing stories which illustrate Biblical principles, sometimes deriving them from old movies, sometimes from current events, or sometimes simply from her own everyday experiences. In fact she continues to learn that if we'll watch carefully and listen to God's Spirit, the Bible and God Himself almost shout aloud! (Romans 1:19-20)

Roberta has been married to Ron Potts for 54 years. The couple currently resides in Scottsdale, Arizona. They have two children and three grandchildren.

robertapotts.com
robertajpottslaw@icloud.com

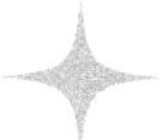

DISCOURAGEMENT IS AN ENEMY THAT YOU MUST FIGHT

Myles Holmes

Discouragement is an enemy that you must FIGHT!

Fight it like you would fight a raging cancer.

Fight it like you would fight a terrorist trying to enter your home.

Fight it like you would fight someone trying to destroy your future and your faith … because that is what is at stake.

Fight it like it is a demon from the pit of hell, because it just might be.

We win with the Word.

We win with the promises of God.

We win by focusing on His Mercy and His Grace!

Do not allow anybody or anything to steal the joy of the Lord which is your strength.

The LORD himself goes before you and will be with you; he will never leave you nor forsake you. Do not be afraid; do not be discouraged.

Deuteronomy 31:8 NIV

Myles Holmes began preaching weekly at 15 years of age, happily married for 42+ years with 5 children, all loving and serving God, and is blessed with 10 grandchildren.

mylesholmes.com
pastor@mylesholmes.com

TRIUMPH AGAINST INSURMOUNTABLE ODDS

John K. Vincent

Now thanks be unto God,
which always causeth us to triumph in Christ,
and maketh manifest the savour of his
knowledge by us in every place.
2 Corinthians 2:14 KJV

Have you ever felt like the wind of life has been knocked out of you? Perhaps you feel spiritually dehydrated and depleted, as though your tank is running on empty? Child of God don't panic. Breathe, and let the Holy Spirit provide rest for your soul.

We live in a very fast-paced world, and many are trying to adjust to the rapid changes in our society. Perhaps the pressures of life are weighing you down heavily, and your faith in God is being stretched. Many today are facing what seem to be insurmountable obstacles and are coping with unhealthy stress and anxiety. It is the plot of the enemy to deceive, discourage, destroy, and conquer our souls, but remember, our help and victory are in the name of Jesus, for He is our all-sufficiency.

Now I realize we do it without even thinking, but have you stopped lately to contemplate ... truly consider just how vital your breathing is for your very survival? Likewise, prayer is essential for spiritual sustenance. It is the key component that allows us to communicate with God, who is the source of all life and strength. Prayer is our spiritual breath that keeps us alive! "Therefore, men ought to always pray and not faint." (Luke 18:1) The Bible says in Romans 8:26, "Likewise the Spirit helps us in our weakness. For we do not know what to pray for as we ought, but the Spirit himself intercedes for us with groanings too deep for words." ESV

There are times in our lives when we don't know what to say or what to do, but the Holy Spirit does. He will always lead and guide us into all truth. The Holy Spirit is God's active power and presence on the earth and dwells in the lives of every believer. Faith in God activates the power to overcome every circumstance in our lives.

I can recall a time in my life when I was mentally and spiritually exhausted. Everything that could go wrong seemed to be happening to me, even with being a born-again and spirit-filled believer. I felt like my world was caving in, and I was about to lose my mind. Outwardly, everything appeared normal, but inwardly, my heart was crushed, and I felt like I could not breathe. My love and faith in God did not exempt me from the challenges of life; I had to confront them face to face. But I discovered how to bounce back and regain my wind. Allow me to share a few things to help you breathe again.

First, acknowledge that amid adversity, you are not alone. God's Spirit is with you and in you, to help you navigate through life's storms. He fights your battles and wins! Sometimes Satan will make you feel as though you have been forsaken by God and left to fend for yourself. But don't accept that lie from the enemy, for God said He will never abandon you. Remember the poem *Footprints in the Sand*? The writer pens in the last stanza. *"I love you and will never leave you. During your trials and testing when you saw only one set of footprints, it was then that I carried you."* God will always be there to see you through your journey.

Second, never isolate yourself from other believers, but remain connected to people who can pour into your life when you are spiritually empty. This can be challenging for some because many are private and don't want others to know about their vulnerable moments. But it's ok, because we all have them! It's alright to solicit the help of your brothers and sisters in Christ. Romans 15:1 NIV says, "We who are strong ought to bear with the failings of the weak and not please ourselves." We are called to help each other in times of need, for there is strength in unity, and there is power in agreement.

Lastly, learn how to maintain a positive and winning attitude! I know at times it may not look like it, and it may not feel like it, but confess that you are a winner anyway! Hold your head up high and begin to thank God for the victory. No matter how painful and emotional the situation may be, remember that your strength and victory are in your obedience to God. In the words of my late father, Bishop Dr. John Vincent Jr., "Son, it's not by your feelings but by your faith."

This is why the apostle Paul expressed gratitude in his letter to the Corinthian church, declaring thanks to God for always causing us to triumph in Christ, despite their trials and persecutions. We, too, must proclaim thanks to God for the triumph! Keep fighting, keep praying, keep trusting, and keep breathing, because this is vital for your soul!

Bishop John Keith Vincent is the founder and Senior Pastor of Greater Compassion Ministries Church of Nashville, Tennessee, the presiding Overseer and founder of United Fellowship Alliance of Ministries, and president of Greater Compassion Community Initiatives. Bishop Vincent is an author, songwriter, recording artist, and visionary leader.

Bishop Vincent holds a bachelor's degree from Oral Roberts University, and an MBA from University of Phoenix, and is currently working on a Doctor of Ministry.

GreaterCompassion.org
greatercompassionministries@gmail.com

HOPE IN ALL SEASONS

Richard Exley

My sister, whom we named Carolyn Faye, was born when I was only nine years old. Her birth was a bittersweet mixture of joy and sorrow. Joy because she was the first daughter after three rowdy boys. Sorrow because she was born hydrocephalic. At birth her head was larger than the rest of her body. She only lived three months. She died just before Christmas of my ninth year. And although she was only with us a short time, I'll never forget her or the hope she brought into our lives.

At first, it was a desperate hope that cried out to God for a miracle—a wordless hope that sometimes found its voice in secret prayer as we wept and begged and pleaded with God for healing. A hope that sometimes found its voice during family devotions when we held hands and agreed as one while Daddy prayed: "God, all things are possible with you. Heal Carolyn." A hope that was sometimes so painful we couldn't speak. It just caught in our throats and felt like a heaviness in our stomachs, a heaviness that never went away. I might forget about Carolyn for a little while in the joy of being nine years old and running at recess. Then at the most unexpected times, it was there. A catch in my throat, a heaviness in my stomach.

And then she died, just a few days before Christmas. I can remember the morning of her death as if it were yesterday. Mother awoke to discover that Carolyn had passed away in her sleep. The doctor arrived and shortly thereafter the mortician came. Then my Aunt Elsie arrived to make breakfast that no one ate. She made breakfast because she wanted to do something and what else could she do but prepare food for us children? I didn't realize it then, but cooking is a commitment to life. With her cooking Aunt Elsie was saying, "Go on, eat! It will be better, you will see. Life will be worth living again. Go ahead, eat your breakfast."

The day of the funeral has been completely erased from my memory leaving me without a single detail. But I do have vivid memories of supper that evening. All the relatives and friends had gone home. Now it was just Mom and Dad and us three boys, and sadness, the ever-present, all-pervading sadness. I remember sitting around the kitchen table with only a small lamp for light. It sat on the kitchen counter in the corner. No overhead light that night—bright lights and grief don't mix. A simple meal and a wordless grief that made eating nearly impossible.

After supper we fled the house, but we could not escape our grief. It filled the car as we drove through the December night looking at Christmas lights, trying to coax even a hint of joy out of a holiday season gone flat. It was my grief-stricken father's way of restoring our faith, his way of reminding us that what happened that first Christmas so long ago changed everything—even Carolyn's death. Now we had a new hope. The hope of being reunited with Carolyn in Heaven where, as John so eloquently writes: "God will wipe away every tear from their eyes. And there'll be no more death or mourning or crying or pain for the old order of things has passed away" (see Revelation 21:4 NIV).

I'm indebted to my parents because they taught me not only to hope, but to trust God in all the seasons of life including the painful season of grief. To trust His craftsmanship even when tragedy seems to make no sense. And to believe that somehow even the most unspeakable loss can be used by God to contribute to our ultimate Christlikeness and can somehow be redeemed and made to hasten the coming of His kingdom in us.

Richard Exley is a seasoned minister with a diversity of experiences. He has been a pastor, a conference and retreat speaker, and a radio broadcaster. He is also the author of more than thirty-five books and hundreds of articles.

To subscribe to his daily One-Minute Devotion, visit
oneminutedevotion.com.

www.youtube.com/@RichardExleyTheStoryteller

LIVING TO SERVE

Neil King

My mom was the epitome of serving others. Whether it was picking up kids for church, taking a meal to people who were in need, or helping others at a moment's notice, that was my mom's mission. I watched her live this verse: "She extends a helping hand to the poor and opens her arms to the needy." Proverbs 31:20 NLT

She was an amazing mother. She taught me everything she knew about Jesus. But at the time, I wasn't very appreciative. I was embarrassed because teenage boys didn't follow their mom around helping others. Looking back, I am so grateful that she set an example of what it means to put others before yourself. Because my mother was so determined to make a difference, she was sometimes labeled as a little eccentric or peculiar. But she didn't care about what some people thought. She cared for the people in need and wanted to make a difference in their lives. If she made your acquaintance, she would find out your birthday and send you both a birthday and Christmas card each year. She wanted you to know that you were valued and loved.

As I grew older, I attended and graduated from Northwest College (now University), then moved to Oklahoma to become a youth pastor. There I met my amazing wife, Jana. Over the years we had three wonderful children. As my kids grew up my mom's health began to decline. At first it was mild but over time it became more progressive. Eventually we had to move Mom into a memory unit.

As I was in Oklahoma and my mom in Idaho, I did not get to connect with her as often as I wanted. One day my sister, Judy, called to let me know that Mother had passed. It was so very difficult to accept, but I was very relieved to know she was in Heaven.

Yet this was not the end of my mother's influence for even in her passing, she would make an eternal impact on someone's life. My brother, Rob, called my sister and I to make arrangements for the funeral. It was agreed that I would share the message.

"Okay, God," I prayed. "You want me to speak, but what am I going to say?" Then I heard inside my heart, "It's the same message you gave long ago at a funeral for a young lady you didn't know." Her father attended the church I pastored at the time. It was a difficult message to give because I did not know the young lady personally, so I had to depend on family members sharing their memories of her with me. One thing I focused on was what this young lady would want to say to us if she could come back and talk to us about eternity and our relationship with God.

Then I heard the Holy Spirit say: "You're going to share this message because someone needs to hear it. This is a very timely message and it's a matter of eternity. If your mother would have passed away earlier, they couldn't have attended the service. If she would have passed away later, they couldn't come. It was only in this time frame that they could come to the service and hear this message so they could have an opportunity to hear, receive and respond."

Here was my mom, already gone from this earth but her legacy spoke of serving, of hope and about a relationship with the Maker of Heaven and Earth.

To me, the most incredible thing is that God used my mom's legacy to share the Gospel with someone on the day of her funeral. His timing is perfect (as always). He's never early nor late. He's always on time and all things work together for His purpose and pleasure.

I'm so grateful that my mom showed me the importance of serving others and lived a life that always pointed to Jesus. May we all be inspired by her life and challenged to follow the example of our Lord and Savior. "For even the Son of Man came not to be served but to serve others and to give his life as a ransom for many." Mark 10:45 NLT

Born and raised in Nampa, Idaho, Neil King graduated from Northwest College (now University). He served both as the youth and senior pastor in various churches and with his wife Jana, now leads The Refuge, a ministry designed to reach and connect with the disenfranchised and the disconnected.

service4theking.com
service4theking@gmail.com

WHEN NOTHING'S HAPPENING, SOMETHING'S HAPPENING!

Stan Toler

University of Illinois football coach Bob Zuppke was famous for his motivational halftime speeches. He really knew how to fire up his teams!

One Saturday afternoon, Zuppke's team was losing and lethargic. Coach Zuppke gave a "win one for the Gipper" kind of speech. And the troops responded excitedly. Dramatically, the coach pointed to the door at the end of the locker room and said, "Now go out there and win this game!"

Emotionally charged, the players jumped up and ran to the door. The first player blasted through the door as several others followed. But there was one problem: It was the wrong door. One by one, they all fell into the swimming pool!

Life is a lot like that! We find a door and charge through it, only to discover it's the wrong door. At other times, we think nothing's happening in our lives. But that's when we should *really* pay attention to what God is doing.

The phrase "When nothing's happening, something's happening!" took on great significance to me on an almost daily basis in my home mission church. I have often confided to friends that I enjoyed this faith-building experience more than any other phase of my ministry.

It constantly required complete and utter dependence on God in the matter of church finances. In other words, we were always *broke!*

On one occasion, I took a step of faith and purchased on credit twenty-two used church pews at a cost of two thousand dollars. That was a wonderful price considering new pews would have cost us approximately eight thousand dollars. There was only one problem—I had no idea on earth how we were going to pay for the pews. After all, our church offerings averaged only one hundred twenty dollars per week. What I didn't know was that God was at work behind the scenes.

I spent a very restless night walking the halls, crying, praying, and wondering why I had just spent two thousand dollars for those pews!

The very next morning, I stopped for my usual cup of coffee at Shoney's and then drove to the post office. There was only one envelope in the mailbox, and it had a window. (Usually, this meant it was a bill!) I got into the car, tossed the letter aside, and drove to my office. (I hate to open bills!) Later in the morning, I decided to open the letter. I was immediately stunned!

It was a letter from the Oldham Little Church Foundation. Two years prior to this faith venture, I had written the Oldham Little Church Foundation requesting financial help with the construction of our church sanctuary. They responded quickly to my letter turning us down. I accepted this disappointment and forgot about the whole situation. Now I was holding a letter from them in my hands:

> *Dear Pastor Toler,*
>
> *Greetings! I am writing to inform you of the decision of Oldham Little Church Foundation board to assist you in your building program. While the enclosed check is small, we trust that it will help you purchase some pulpit furniture. Enclosed is a check for $2,000.*

As I have reflected on this incident, I am reminded that God's timing is always perfect. He knows what we need and when we need it. Personally, I have on occasion wished that He would work with my time schedule. But this I know: God is never late, and He never fails! Never!

StanToler.com

MIND THE GAP

Michael McGinnis

On my first trip to the United Kingdom, I experienced a myriad of new things. I traveled primarily for academic aspirations – studying the life and work of C. S. Lewis and friends, in particular J.R.R. Tolkien, and I presented a lecture at St. Aldates Parish Centre in Oxford. In order to reach Oxford, I had to travel first to London. London has one of the largest public transport networks in the world and I rode the London Underground, also referred to as the Tube. At one particular train stop, I visited Paddington Station where the fictional character Paddington Bear made his first big-screen debut appearance in London.

There is, just before stepping onto the Tube, a painted white sign beyond the yellow line on the staging platform which reads, "Mind the Gap." While entering and exiting this underground metro system, the automatic voice announcement continually reminds riders to mind the gap, indicating the importance of watching one's step so as not to fall through the space between the train and the platform.

There are aspects of our lives similar to travel and adventuring, a real journey of sorts, offering both progress and delays, oftentimes full of signs, sometimes cautions, and even warnings, meant for our good as we traverse successful living on this earth. The temptation is to ignore directional signposts along the way in life, marriage, family, and vocation, asserting that we know more or best. Regularly ignoring these notifications and attempting isolated and independent living can cause one to regrettably step into the gap, resulting in a fall and injury, bringing about a deeper level of trouble. But it does not have to be this way.

The human experience is more about the journey than a series of landmark events. We are meant to learn and grow becoming the type of person God wants us to become. God gives us grace, the power to change, through a process called discipleship. It does not occur overnight. In his book, *Atomic Habits*, James Clear suggests that "the most powerful outcomes are delayed." (20) One of the hardest adjustments for most is gaining patience and enduring the mundane periods of living and learning.

Life is not meant to be lived or measured by the major events, but by how we live day in and day out. The best things are more likely to occur during the waiting or in the crucial middle moments and experiences. This is where the people, places, and provisions for the next event will most certainly appear. The best use of one's transitional or gap time is preparation. Preparation time is never lost time, but worrying about the future or longing for another day causes us to miss the beauty of the present, and to stress over things that may or may not ever happen.

We all tend to love the bigger, main events in life – graduating high school or college, gaining a new job or promotion, getting married or having children, and even conquering endurance races, grueling challenge courses, or other competitions. But what about the daily grind – the times when we feel trapped in the gap or in between all the excitement, and forced to wait or left on the sidelines and feeling alone? There are at least three things I would like to offer here to be of help to you. These are proven practices and principles of understanding that can get you through the commonplace and uneventful spaces.

The first principle is to seek the Lord for His wisdom and guidance. "If you need wisdom, ask our generous God, and He will give it to you. He will not rebuke you for asking" (James 1:5, NLT). He knows everything and we do not, so reach out by reaching up and He will reach into your life to help you.

Secondly, avoid navigating life's journey alone and apart from others who can help. Christian community is God's design, and the local church is one of the ways in which He surrounds us with His love and healthy guidance and encouragement. While we are waiting for the next big thing, there are people God wants us to receive from and others in whom He wants us to invest. The answer you are looking for may be just one Sunday observance of the Sabbath away.

Finally, get ready for the ride of your life and prepare for the next arriving train called purpose. You will have to mind the gap. Simply step over obstacles, hop, and hold on. In most European travel, passengers are not considered rude when pressing their way onto a train, in fact, if they do not, they will likely miss their train or painfully get stuck in the automated closing doorway. Trust me, I know!

While boarding an overcrowded train with my family, one of my children hopped ahead of me and as I stepped on board, two of my family members were a bit behind and pressing to reach the door. At that moment, as the bell rang, I had to make a decision as I felt the door close heavily on me, not once but two then three times. I remained in the doorway while my wife and our other child fought their way on board. Though it was painful and a potentially embarrassing experience, we all made the train together. When preparation meets opportunity, remarkable things can happen. Unfortunately, when the opportunity train arrives, we find ourselves unprepared and wanting. Do not miss the next train and destination God has planned for you (Jeremiah 29:11). Prepare now for your purpose.

While international travel can be lively and enjoyable, it can be quite tiresome and stressful at the same time. The adventure God has planned for your life is better than you may think. Seek God's wisdom and vision for your life. Stay connected to a loving, Christian community and prepare like there is no tomorrow. If you happen to miss the next train, you may have to wait a while. Just be sure to mind the gap when it comes.

Clear, James. Atomic habits: an easy and proven way to build good habits and break bad ones. New York: Avery, 2018.

"Paddington." IMDb, January 16, 2015. https://www.imbd.com/title/tt1109624/.

Mike McGinnis is a writer, classically trained Christian educator, podcaster, investor, and lifelong learner. He hosts *The Christian Influence Podcast with Mike McGinnis.* Mike graduated from College of the Ozarks with a Biblical and Theological Studies degree and completed a Master of Organizational Leadership program at Evangel University. Mike is currently enrolled in a doctoral program.

Mike on LinkedIn at www.linkedin.com/in/michael-mcginnis-mol-b77003353

Michael.mcginnis3030@gmail.com

Photos by Michael McGinnis

WE ALL NEED FOUR GOOD FRIENDS

Chuck Burton

One of my favorite Bible stories is when Jesus taught in the crowded house in Capernaum (Mark 2:3-13 ESV). Four guys tore the roof off of the house and lowered a guy down in front of Jesus.

My assumption is that the disabled guy knew or was friends with the four guys.

Here are some rabbit trails we could chase down:

1. Did they fix the roof afterward?
2. Why do "religious" people even get a voice?
3. Did the homeowner gladly fix the roof himself and count it joy that this healing event happened in his house?

Here is my point…

We all need four good friends.

Roof tearing-off friends.

Carry me around when I need it…tear the roof off…get me in front of Jesus friends.

Chuck Burton is a pastor and lives in Tulsa, Oklahoma.

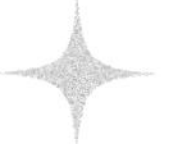

MY EXPERIENCE ASSISTING PASTOR JOHN OSTEEN

David Ingles

After meeting John and Dodie Osteen, it was a continual blessing hearing them speak, teach, and love on people. Several times Brother Osteen called on me. "Brother David, this is Brother Osteen. I need you to come and pastor Lakewood for me." It was usually two Sundays plus mid-week services. This gave him almost three weeks to reach out to the people of India or the Philippine Islanders.

He would say, "You can stay in a hotel, a motel, or you can stay in the mobile home here behind the church." I would take my family, and we would stay in the mobile home.

On one particular occasion, Pastor John asked me to sing and teach several nights. One morning as we passed each other in the hallway we just nodded and walked on. From down the hallway he yelled back, "Brother David, just go where you have favor."

That anointed exhortation has served me numerous times.

"JUST GO WHERE YOU HAVE FAVOR."

davidinglesmusic.org
oasisnetwork.org

LIVING THE DREAM

Jeffrey Brucculeri

I realize the term "Living the Dream" has become a bit of a cliché. If you ask someone, "How are you doing?" they may reply, "Just living the dream."

However, they don't always mean that. But, if you ask me and I respond that way, I mean it.

You see, I learned a long time ago that one's dreams can really become reality, and I'm blessed to say that many of mine certainly have.

When I was a kid, I had a dream of someday being on radio and television, I wanted to be a professional mascot, and I wanted to work for and travel with the World-Famous Harlem Globetrotters.

I've accomplished all of that and more.

However, none of it came easy. I learned there were certain steps I needed to take along the way to achieve those dreams and turn them into reality. I also learned that some dreams just never come true.

Commit to the Lord whatever you do, and he will establish your plans. Proverbs 16:3 NIV

To achieve success, you may need to take risks. Most people fear taking risks because they're afraid they might fail. Most people are afraid to fail because they're worried about what people will say about them. Most people are worried about what others will say about them because they suffer from low self-esteem. So, the secret to success is to find a way to raise your self-esteem.

One way to do that is to believe that God has placed this dream in your heart for a reason and that He will open the appropriate doors along the way to achieving your goal. Once you realize that, you can pursue the appropriate steps with confidence and faith that you *will* achieve what was set before you.

Dreaming about something isn't enough though. You must decide to take action; get up and get going!

You've heard the saying, "Most people fail because they fail to start." Boy, is that true. Once you have a dream in your heart and you begin to act on it, you need to have a clear vision of where you want to end up. If you don't know where you want to go, any road will take you there. If you want to travel east but you're on a north-south route, you will never get to your destination.

You must be willing to pivot, take a turn in a different direction to find the best path to reach your destination. You need to be able to see where it is you're going and imagine what it's going to look like when you get there.

You should have a clear idea of what your purpose is. I was 30 years old when I learned that my purpose is to educate, inform, and entertain people. Ironically, I was already living out my purpose and didn't realize it. At the time, I hosted a four-hour talk show every weekday and I was broadcasting sports. Those were the things that fired me up and regardless of how little I was getting paid, I enjoyed the work and was very passionate about what I did. I was educating, informing and entertaining people through radio and television.

If you achieve your dream, you must consider three factors; will it fire you up so much that you are excited to get out of bed in the morning and begin doing what you do best? Will it serve others? Does it align with your purpose and God's plan for your life?

If it doesn't it will fail, but you shouldn't see it as the end of the world. Nobody wants to pursue the dream of becoming an acrobat, only to find out later they are afraid of heights.

You may encounter some roadblocks along the way, so ask yourself, "What is my motivation?"

People set goals and then find out they just don't have enough lasting motivation to continue. One way to avoid this is to identify a motivator; something that will keep you moving forward even when things become difficult, because they will. Many people begin with a great dream or plan but once they encounter some rough spots in the road, they give up.

Your motivator could be a particular person, an experience you've had, or a statement that will give you the fuel you need to continue down the road to success.

"Ability is what you're capable of doing. Motivation determines what you do. Attitude determines how well you do it." Lou Holtz (former Notre Dame Football Coach)

Stop the negative thinking and begin to think more positively about yourself and what you have. Remind yourself of all the successes, the good things you've accomplished and the lessons you've learned from the mistakes.

Take delight in the LORD, and he will give you the desires of your heart. Psalm 37:4 NIV

God never promised that all our dreams would come true, but as we seek Him, and understand His plan for our life, those dreams can become reality, and that's what really Living the Dream is all about.

Jeff is an accomplished trumpet player with over 45 years' experience. He has used his talents to minister in many different settings, both as a solo artist and as the lead trumpet player with several bands, and he has performed the National Anthem prior to numerous sports events. He has authored two books and has recorded three solo albums. Jeff has been featured on the Christian Television Network and appeared on the FOX Television show *SuperHuman*. Jeff has appeared as an actor in dozens of corporate videos, commercials and movies.

Since 2008, Jeff has traveled on more than a dozen mission trips and has ministered in seven foreign countries. With his experience as a radio and television broadcaster and his unique sense of humor, Jeff is able to communicate to a wide range of audiences. He's a member of the Christian Comedy Association and has toured as the announcer for the World-Famous Harlem Globetrotters.

Jeff is a graduate of Oral Roberts University. He and his wife, Colleen, live in Broken Arrow, Oklahoma. They have two children and two grandchildren.

jeffbministries.com
info@jeffbministries.com

HOW IS YOUR FOUNDATION?

Carl Fauth

During my college years, I took advantage of every fall, spring, and summer break to return to my hometown in Montana to work. I was working toward a ministry degree in Canada, because I had no work permit or visa in Canada and could not work, it left me to work long hours to raise money while back in the States.

One particular construction project I was asked to build, against my recommendation, was a boardwalk and roof across the front of the Phillips County Museum. The boardwalk was not the issue, but the all-wood slat roof would be. The museum did not want a shingle or metal roof but rather a bare wood slat (which I knew would definitely rot).

During the construction process, I chose to go the extra mile and prepare not only for the slat roof, but the next roof that would be installed in the future. About ten years later, while driving through my hometown, something caught my eye: a new metal roof on the front of the museum.

Similar stories should be shared in our spiritual lives. Many times, we work hard to help others set a firm foundation that will be the base for future growth, success, and upgrades.

Jesus taught us to build foundations on solid rock, so that when the rain came or the wind blew, the house (or in the museum's case the roof) would stand firm.

Anyone who listens to my teaching and follows it is wise, like a person who builds a house on solid rock. Though the rain comes in torrents and the floodwater rises and the winds beat against that house, it won't collapse because it is built on bedrock.

But anyone who hears my teaching and doesn't obey it is foolish, like a person who builds a house on sand. When the rains and floods come and the winds beat against that house, it will collapse with a mighty crash.
Matthew 7:24-27 NLT

How is your foundation? Are you helping build the foundations of others? Can the next person build on them?

Carl Fauth has served as a Worship and Tech Pastor for more than twenty years, dedicating his life to equipping and encouraging others in their faith journey. He and his wife are raising three boys and currently serve together at Life360 Chesterfield in Springfield, Missouri.

In addition to his ministry work, Carl has a background in Human Resources and has been nominated for Springfield's Top Human Resources Professional Award. He is also a Certified Great Game of Business Coach, helping organizations thrive through open-book management. In 2022, Carl was honored as one of Springfield Business Journal's 40 Under 40 for his leadership and community impact.

Carl is passionate about helping people grow spiritually, build healthy relationships, and live with purpose.

carlfauth@gmail.com

Photo by Nancy Fauth

GARAGED

Roberta Roberts Potts

For many years my husband, Ron, and I owned a very large German Shepherd dog named "Bigboy." The good news is that he was very well-trained and thankfully, wonderfully obedient. While he loved both of us, Bigboy definitely looked to Ron as his master.

One Saturday afternoon we decided to have a backyard barbecue for our friends. Since it was a nice cool, fall day, we decided to put Bigboy in the garage for the afternoon while our guests were there. We knew it would not be too hot nor too cool for the dog in our garage. We carefully placed both food and water for Bigboy, a nice cushy rug for him to lay upon and he obediently and quietly remained there during the course of the party.

Everything worked out great except that afterwards, we were so busy cleaning up, and so tired after doing so, well I'm ashamed to admit that we forgot about our poor dog still being held captive in our garage! Once we realized our mistake, Ron rushed to open the garage door, wondering why Bigboy hadn't made a sound. Was he dead? Had he somehow escaped from the garage? Of course we both felt horribly guilty about forgetting him.

But surprise, surprise, Ron opened the door and there was Bigboy, no worse for wear. Of course he was *very* happy to see his master and extremely relieved to finally be allowed out of the garage. Ron was treated to a huge dose of licks and all was well.

Now some dogs would have gone crazy, howled, thrown a fit, carried a grudge, and I don't know what all, but not Bigboy. And I believe there is something to be learned here. Of course our God never *forgets* us, but there are times when it certainly *seems* that He does. When Joseph was thrown into a pit, sold by his own brothers, betrayed by a cruel, designing woman and generally mistreated by so many, all that time, God was in fact carrying out His indescribably stupendous plan for Joseph. It only *seemed* Joseph had been forgotten.

So what are we to do during those times when we *feel* God has forgotten us? I believe *our* Master expects us to remain calm as Bigboy did in our garage that day. Not inclined to worry. Relaxed and believing his master would let him out at the proper time. Knowing his master and happy he could trust him in every situation. Of course you may know the rest of the story — but just to refresh our memories, Joseph ended up running all of Egypt and saving what would become the entire nation of Israel. Oh no, God hadn't forgotten him, not hardly. The Lord was training Joseph, preparing him for his future. (See Genesis 37, 39-50) Yes it took many years, but the day came when the Lord made this perfectly clear to Joseph. He told his brothers: "You intended to harm me, but God intended it all for good. He brought me to this position so I could save the lives of many people." (Genesis 50:20 NLT)

And when you think about it, really consider it, how could we ever think *our* Master would forget us and simply leave us in that garage—lonely and forsaken? Consider the things God has done for *you*. Yes, humans forget but our God NEVER does that. No matter what it may seem to us, the Word of God clearly tells us that He will **never** leave us nor forsake us! (from Hebrews 13:5)

While at times you may feel as if you're the one stuck in the garage with everyone else having lots of fun, enjoying a great big party right next door — and you're left out, while you may *feel* like the forgotten one, it's never *really* that way. As the scripture stated no less than three separate times about Joseph, God is *with* you! (See Genesis 39:2, 3, and 21.)

Jesus is referred to as "Emmanuel" meaning "God is with us" (Isaiah 7:14 NLT; Matthew 1:23 KJV) and *your* Master absolutely never forgets His own.

So no need to "bark," no need to whine. No need to cry and feel sorry for yourself. Trust your Master. All is well.

For 25 years, Roberta practiced as an attorney in the State of Oklahoma representing individuals who were injured in motor vehicle accidents. As the younger daughter of Oral Roberts, Roberta grew up watching her father preaching and praying for the sick in vast healing crusades. Assisting hurting people not only seemed a natural extension of her father's healing ministry, but it also gave her an opening to pray for the sick as well.

Since that time she has written a book about her father (*My Dad, Oral Roberts*), assisted others with their writing projects and composed a number of devotional and teaching articles as well. For several years she has also assisted her pastor with sermon illustrations. Her newest project is Roberta's Research, reaching out to assist other pastors and authors as well.

She enjoys writing stories which illustrate Biblical principles, sometimes deriving them from old movies, sometimes from current events, or sometimes simply from her own everyday experiences. In fact she continues to learn that if we'll watch carefully and listen to God's Spirit, the Bible and God Himself almost shout aloud! (Romans 1:19-20)

Roberta has been married to Ron Potts for 54 years. The couple currently resides in Scottsdale, Arizona. They have two children and three grandchildren.

robertapotts.com
robertajpottslaw@icloud.com

SURPRISING SUPERNATURAL SUPPLY

Myles Holmes

My wife and I had been married for a few months and were traveling in evangelism. Itinerant ministry meant that we had no regular income; we were just trusting God for His provision as we traveled.

While residing in the basement of Valerie's parents' home in Toronto, Canada, we received an invitation from a pastor in Massachusetts for a weekend of ministry.

We traveled over 500 miles by car and ministered on Friday night, twice on Saturday and twice on Sunday, preaching and singing. We gave our best and felt that God was glorified, seeing souls saved and believers blessed.

As we were leaving Monday morning, the pastor handed us an envelope thanking us for our ministry. A few miles down the road Valerie opened the envelope and we were shocked that there were two $20 bills, $40. We had 513 miles to return by car. This was 1983, but $40 wouldn't even pay the gas to get us back to Canada.

We were devastated, pulled to the side of the road, sat for a few moments and decided to pray. "God we don't know what to do, but we're trusting You... Whatever we need to learn, please teach us, but help us because we need to get back home."

To say we were desperate would be an understatement because at this point we didn't even have a credit card, and not enough cash in my wallet to buy food and gas to get home. Just enough money to get a few miles down the road and a motel for one night.

The next morning we got up and drove slowly, enjoyed some of New England, got a cheap lunch and kept driving. Later that afternoon I suggested to Valerie that we go to church if we could find anyone who had a Tuesday evening service. She agreed, and we found an Assembly of God church open.

We walked in and an usher was so glad to see a young couple, he warmly welcomed us and asked us where we were from and what brought us to church. We told him we were evangelists just heading home and he asked us if we had a musical ministry. I affirmed that and he asked us to please get ready to sing and he would let the pastor know we were there.

I went out to the car and picked up a cassette tape for accompaniment, went into the church and the pastor called us up to sing. To this day I wish that I could remember what we sang, but that is lost to memory.

It was a small crowd on a Tuesday night Bible study and prayer service, not an overly memorable service, but what happened that night has marked our ministry for more than 42 years.

As we were leaving, the pastor called us over in the foyer and said the Lord told him to bless us as we were starting out in ministry. He handed us an envelope, we thanked him and prayed over him then left in our car. Valerie opened the envelope, and we were shocked as she counted out twenty $20 bills. A $400 blessing for one song! More than enough to make up for the previous church's lack of blessing.

Again, we had to pull the car over to the side of the road, but this time crying and rejoicing, thanking God for His right-on-time, miraculous, supernatural supply.

That has been the story for the rest of our life in full-time ministry over 42 years. Whether traveling in evangelism, pastoring three different churches in two different nations, or in years of television ministry, God has always brought enough, and then more than enough, right on time to meet our needs and to prove that He knew exactly where we were and that He was our supply—no man and no organization—God and God alone is our Provider.

Miracle after miracle, blessing after blessing has been our story.

We have always tithed, $4 from the $40 and $40 from the $400, and given above that, and that's why God has always met our needs.

Philippians 4:19 still promises "God will supply all your needs according to His riches in glory by Christ Jesus." NKJV.

Malachi 3:10 "Bring all the tithes into the storehouse, That there may be food in My house, And try Me now in this," says the Lord of hosts, "If I will not open for you the windows of Heaven, and pour out for you such blessing that there will not be room enough to receive it." NKJV

Myles Holmes began preaching weekly at 15 years of age, happily married for 42+ years with 5 children, all loving and serving God, and is blessed with 10 grandchildren.

mylesholmes.com
pastor@mylesholmes.com

RESOURCES

I have been enriched by working with scores of gifted and Spirit-anointed people who have changed my life. While it is impossible and impractical to list all of them, I thought you would enjoy knowing these people and their products and services.

The following pages are a tribute to these friends, as they have helped me become the person I am today.

Inclusion in this section is solely at the author's discretion. No warranties are expressed or implied.

When You Lose Someone You Love
20th Anniversary Edition

Written as a series of heart-to-heart letters, best-selling author Richard Exley draws on years of pastoral ministry to give you the comfort of a true friend. You'll draw reassurance from the real experiences of others who have faced devastating loss, and begin to see how hope can one day triumph over grief. Most importantly, you will discover how the mercy and grace of God provide the promise of eternal life.

Your most difficult questions -- including your doubts about God's goodness, or perhaps His very existence, are fearlessly addressed. Realistic and empathetic insights will enable you to trust God with your loss even though it seems to make no sense.

Long after the flowers have faded and the sympathy cards are tucked away, "When You Lose Someone You Love" will still be speaking peace and promise to your heart. An expression of continuing concern and comfort, it is sure to be your most welcome companion during your journey through grief.

Order from the author:
RichardExleyMinistries.org

My Dad, Oral Roberts

Roberta Roberts Potts

He was born at the height of the War to End All Wars, in the little town of Ada, Oklahoma. By the time Oral Roberts passed from this life in 2009, American evangelicalism became a truly global endeavor, due in no small part to this faith-healer who began his ministry in tent revivals.

Now, his daughter, Roberta Roberts Potts has penned a loving, inside view of the man and his ministry. Filled with anecdotes and observations about one of the world's most famous preachers, *My Dad, Oral Roberts* serves as the only biography of Granville Oral Roberts from his family.

Full of wonderful photos and memories—both poignant and happy—*My Dad, Oral Roberts* is a truly fascinating read, and a wonderful testament to a life of faith.

Order from the author:

www.robertapotts.com/my-book/

Eric Smith's books are available in paperback and Kindle at Amazon: https://shorturl.at/z5ot3

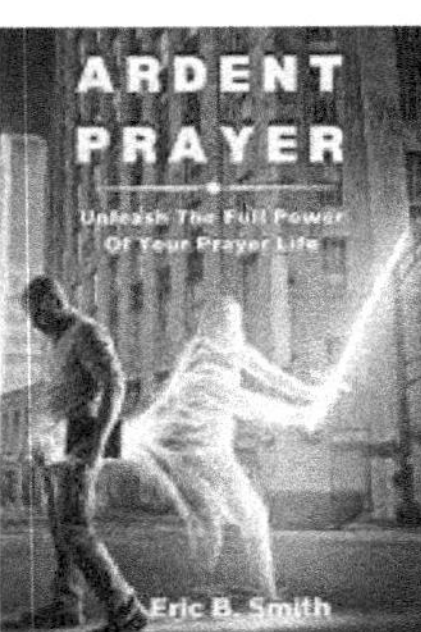

GREG WHEAT
FROM
HERE
TO
THERE
GETTING FROM WHERE YOU ARE TO WHERE YOU ARE MEANT TO BE.
FOREWORD BY RUSS TAFF
A 6-time Grammy and 16-time Dove awards winner.

Factual Accounts of
Courage, Hope, and Inspiration
Told in Story, Song, and Scripture
MOVE UP!
DON'T GIVE UP!
THOMAS HARRISON
Foreword by Roberta Roberts Potts

OASIS
RADIO NETWORK
www.oasisnetwork.org

Media Embassy LLC
Communicating Your Message
MediaEmbassy.com

MY FAVORITE REFERENCES

Exley, R. (2013). *When You Lose Someone You Love.* David C. Cook.

Exley, R. (2017). *Dancing in the Dark.* Word & Spirit Publishing.

Green, D. (2017). *Giving It All Away...and Getting It All Back Again.* Zondervan.

Green, D., & Merrill, D. (2010). *More Than A Hobby: how a $600 start-up became America's home and craft superstore.* Thomas Nelson.

Hansen, B. (2015). *Unoffendable: how just one change can make all of life better.* W Publishing Group, An Imprint of Thomas Nelson.

Harrison, T. (2021). *Move Up! Don't Give Up! Factual accounts of courage, hope, and inspiration told in story, song, and scripture.* DustJacket.

Harrison, T. (2026). *Oxygen For The Soul: Life Is Too Short To Be Discouraged.* DustJacket.

Holmes, M. (2015). *Fasting for Breakthrough.* CreateSpace.

Jeary, T. (2009). *Purpose-Filled Presentations.* Standard Publishing. *

Jeary, T., Dower, K., & Fishman, J. E. (2005). *Life Is A Series Of Presentations: eight ways to inspire, inform, and influence anyone, anywhere, anytime.* Fireside.

Lencioni, P. (2016). *The Truth About Employee Engagement: a fable about addressing the three root causes of job misery*. Jossey-Bass, Wiley.

Logue, M., & Conradi, P. J. (2010). *The King's Speech*. Sterling. **

Potts, R.R. (2011). *My Dad, Oral Roberts*. Icon.

Smith, E. B. (2023). *Set Free*. Independently Published.

Toler, S. (2009). *The Inspirational Speaker's Resource*. Beacon Hill Press.

Toler, S. (2011). *Stan Toler's Practical Guide For Pastoral Ministry*. Wesleyan Pub. House.

Wheat, G. (2025). *From Here To There: getting from where you are to where you are meant to be*. DustJacket.

*I was a contributing author to Scenario 9.

**The Kings Speech (movie) is inspirational. Please note, it is rated R for one scene of foul language.

Note: The references listed above are a tribute to friends and authors as they have helped me become the person I am today. Inclusion in this section is solely at my discretion. Financial consideration was neither extended nor accepted. No warranties are expressed or implied.

ABOUT THE AUTHOR

Thomas Harrison, Ph.D.

Thomas Harrison has managed radio and television stations in Arkansas and Oklahoma. He was awarded Telly and Angel Awards for his work in media.

Harrison is an ordained minister and has served in ministry positions (associate pastor, interim pastor, discipleship pastor) for churches and ministries in both Missouri, and Oklahoma.

As a community leader, Thomas has served as President of the Broken Arrow, Oklahoma Ministerial Alliance, and is a graduate of the Citizens Police Academy of Broken Arrow, Oklahoma. He serves as a board member of Ignite Church, Norman, Oklahoma, and advisory elder for The Refuge, Wagoner, Oklahoma.

Dr. Harrison has served as an instructor and/or academic administrator for Oral Roberts University, Central Bible College, Evangel University, University of Phoenix, and others.

A first-generation college student, Harrison attended Oral Roberts University (B.S. Media), the University of Oklahoma (M.A. Journalism), Saint Louis University (Ph.D.) and University of Phoenix (Professional Certificate: Digital Marketing).

His work has been featured in *Wall Street Journal, Tulsa World, The Oklahoman, CBN News (700 Club), Oasis Radio Network, Tulsa Beacon Radio, LeSEA Network, Daystar*, and scores of media outlets and internet podcasts.

He is the author of *Move Up! Don't Give Up! Factual Accounts of Courage, Hope, and Inspiration Told in Story, Song, and Scripture* and *Oxygen For The Soul: Life Is Too Short To Be Discouraged* both published by DustJacket Press, available in a variety of formats from Amazon.com.

Thomas and Kathy Harrison have been married for more than forty-six years and make their home in the Ozarks along with their miniature dachshund, Jasmine.

You may contact Dr. Harrison at **Thomas@mediaembassy.com**

www.ingramcontent.com/pod-product-compliance
Lightning Source LLC
LaVergne TN
LVHW010054110826
845155LV00028B/331